The Reign of Terror: A Narrative of Facts Concerning Ex-Governor Eyre, George William Gordon, and the Jamaica Atrocities

Henry Bleby

THE REIGN OF TERROR

EYRE.

GORDON.

RAMSAY.

RUINS OF MORANT BAY COURT HOUSE.

MORRIS.

ADCOCK. NELSON.

CULLEN.

THE REIGN OF TERROR:

A NARRATIVE OF FACTS

CONCERNING

EX-GOVERNOR EYRE, GEORGE WILLIAM GORDON,

AND

THE JAMAICA ATROCITIES.

BY

HENRY BLEBY,

AUTHOR OF THE " DEATH STRUGGLES OF SLAVERY," " SCENES IN THE
CARIBBEAN SEA," " PREDESTINATION NOT FATALISM," " TRUE AND
FALSE APOSTLES," " THE WICKEDNESS AND DOOM
OF THE PAPACY," ETC., ETC.

" The hell-like saturnalia of martial law."—MR. ROUNDELL, Secretary to the Royal
Commission to Jamaica.

LONDON.

1868.

LONDON:

PRINTED BY WILLIAM NICHOLS,

46, HOXTON SQUARE.

PREFACE.

THE following pages are designed to exhibit the truth in defence of a deeply wronged and slandered people. Wide-spread misapprehension and ignorance prevail concerning the disturbances in Jamaica in 1865, and the measures adopted by the local authorities with respect to them. Few persons have a correct idea of the facts associated with the outbreak, or of the atrocities which were practised during martial law. The writer feels it to be due to the murdered members of the Church he belongs to, whose blood still cries from the ground; to the black and coloured inhabitants of the British West India Colonies, who are a meek, long-suffering, and forgiving race, and not the monsters of cruelty and vengeance they have been represented; to the Missionary Churches of the West Indies; and, above all, to the cause of truth and righteousness, to give to the religious public such a brief, consecutive narrative as may help those who are candid and right-minded to arrive at right conclusions concerning the tragedy, and the several parties who were prominently concerned therein. Such a narrative will be found in this publication; which, it is hoped, will tend to neutralize, in some measure, the great wrong that was done, when some Christian Ministers in Jamaica, panic-stricken, and ignorant of many of the horrible deeds which had been enacted, forgot what was due to the people of their charge, and appended their signatures to complimentary addresses to men whose proceedings have been shown, by the results of official investigation, to be deserving of the utmost reprobation. Those who desire more fully to know the details of this tale of horror, will do well to read the " *Parliamentary Blue Books* " relating to the Jamaica disturbances, and the inquiry of the Royal Commissioners concerning them; " *Jamaica and the Colonial Office*," by the Hon. G. Price; and the series of " *Papers by the Jamaica Committee*."

The title which this pamphlet bears has been adopted, because it is descriptive of the state of feeling that prevailed in Jamaica in the latter part of 1865, in consequence of the sanguinary tyranny of the authorities, and which even yet is far from having passed away. Many persons feared to write to their friends, because letters were broken open and in some cases stopped altogether by the Government; and multitudes, especially amongst the more intelligent and respectable coloured people, were afraid to speak upon passing events to each other, or whisper their thoughts in the privacy of their own domestic circle; lest, being overheard, they should be dragged to prison or to the gallows, or subjected, without trial, to the torture of " the wire-tailed cat." It is not too much to say that, for many months, the whole population of the land were paralysed wit " *terror.*"

CONTENTS.

THE REIGN OF TERROR.

CHAPTER I.

The philanthropy and the Christianity of Britain suffered a sad eclipse in the events which transpired in Jamaica during the latter part of 1865; and the honour of the British army and navy was shamefully sullied by the brutality of military and naval officers, and the readiness with which they lent themselves to perform deeds of cruelty, to which we can scarcely find a parallel amongst any savage people on the face of the earth. Englishmen felt the blush of shame and indignation mantling their cheeks, at the dishonour done to themselves and their country, when they saw one filling the proud position of their Queen's representative coming down from his high station, eagerly thrusting aside the policeman, and invading his office and duty, to capture and punish a political opponent, and also personally superintending and taking part in the cruel death of a poor Negro, who in the silence of the night is dragged from his home, and, after a wretched mockery of a trial which is a burlesque upon the administration of justice, is at once put to death with circumstances of revolting inhumanity. The shame and indignation thus felt was aggravated, as they read of men commanding vessels in Her Majesty's navy, performing the degrading duties of the hangman; and

B

others, bearing the commission of colonel or holding other rank in the army, servilely obeying orders which it was an outrage against decency and humanity to issue, and an insult to British officers to receive, and revelling with savage glee in the slaughter of defenceless and unresisting men.   It is not to the honour of Britain that many, associated with the upper classes of society, have put themselves forward to shield the evil-doers in this case from the consequences of their misdeeds, and prevent that full and impartial inquiry which offended justice and humanity demanded when the character of the nation was so seriously compromised.   It relieves in some measure, though it fails to vindicate, the sullied honour of the nation, that the force of public opinion compelled a reluctant Government to dismiss Governor Eyre from the position he had dishonoured, and appoint a Commission to bring to light the true facts of the case ; also that the philanthropy and justice of the nation, represented by the Jamaica Committee, have, by forcing some of the guilty parties to the bar of justice, called forth that lucid and elaborate charge of Lord Chief Justice Cockburn, in the case of Nelson and Brand, which leaves a lasting stigma upon both branches of the public service, disgraced by the inhumanity of these officers, and brands ex-Governor Eyre with a degree of culpability which few men would like to bear with them to the grave and beyond it, as he will not fail to do.

The administration of Mr. Eyre is not likely to be soon forgotten in Jamaica.   A few panic-stricken women, and some feeble-minded men——too feeble to be capable of forming an opinion themselves—may laud him as having saved them from a variety of perils which had no existence except in their own over-excited imagination ; but all right-minded persons will reprobate his government, as by far the most disastrous and oppressive with which Jamaica has ever been afflicted. Unlettered and ignorant as most of the Negroes in Jamaica are, they are fully awake to the fact that life and liberty were never more insecure within her shores than when they lay at the mercy of Mr. Eyre and his advisers. Many persons endeavour to palliate the faults of the ex-Governor, and find an excuse for the atrocities committed and sanctioned under his administration, by urging that he was misled and acted under the influence of bad advisers. Were it even so, that would be no apology for such deeds as were perpetrated by him, and under his direction. He had no right, as the representative of England's Queen, to put his office in commission, so as to divest himself of the responsibilities inherently belonging to his position; nor could he in fact do so. The moral responsibility of all the murders of Negroes, and burning of Negro cottages, and the innumerable outrages against person, life, and property that took place during the reign of terror called martial law, rests upon his head; and if mistaken men combine to screen him from legal punishment, his wrong-doing will not fail to be remembered when the Just and Holy One shall make inquisition for blood. Mr. Eyre was misled less by evil advisers than by his own prejudices and passions. His appointment was a mistake. He was an unfit man to be placed in such a high position, and to exercise such powers as those intrusted to him. His developments prove him to be a man of the most ordinary intellectual abilities, and also defective in some of those higher moral qualities without which no man is eminently great or good. Let the character of ex-Governor Eyre, as exhibited in his administration of the government of Jamaica, be analysed, and there will be found a deplorable abnegation of the nobler elements which constitute the leading characteristics of a truly great and estimable public man, such as the late Lord Metcalfe, who for several years occupied the same position, and commanded in a high degree the confidence and esteem of all the inhabitants of Jamaica as their friend and benefactor. Much has been said in the way of apology concerning the earlier developments of Mr. Eyre, and the amiable qualities he has exhibited on some occasions, his religious habits, &c. It may be all true; and just as much may be said with regard to many who have in the end stood out before the world shocking the sensibilities of men, when all that had hitherto appeared so fair and estimable in them was overcast and obliterated by the dark cloud of crime. For aught we know to the contrary, Mr. Eyre as an Australian explorer may have been as blameless as other travellers; and in his subsequent career as a colonial governor or sub-governor he may have kept himself from blameable excesses, because no powerful temptations presented themselves. But when the time of severe trial came to him in Jamaica, and he was placed in circumstances which demanded the exercise of high and noble qualities in the head of the government, to control and direct the current of passing events to a wise and favourable issue, then he signally failed; it became painfully evident that the commanding capabilities which the crisis required in the man at the helm of public affairs were mournfully lacking; and he stood revealed, the unenviable bearer of the responsibilities attached to him in the charge of Chief Justice Cockburn, and author of what Mr. Roundell, the secretary of the Jamaica Royal Commission, appropriately designates *"the hell-like saturnalia of martial law."*

By the evidence taken on oath by the Royal Com-

missioners to whom the important task of investigation
was intrusted, and who were armed with authority to
compel the attendance and testimony of witnesses of all
classes, from ex-Governor Eyre downwards, it is clearly
shown that the outbreak at Morant Bay, in the parish
of St. Thomas-in-the-East, was simply a local riot,
magnified by the craven fears of the civil and military
authorities of the island into "*a dreadful rebellion*,"
and made the occasion and pretext for shocking excesses,
to which it will be difficult to find a parallel in British
colonial history. During the dark days of slavery,
panics not unfrequently occurred in Jamaica, proving
the chronic state of fear and apprehension in which the
colonists lived, while they reaped the profits of a system fraught with cruel injustice and oppression to the
African race, so long trodden down and plundered by
the professedly Christian nations of Europe.   These
were sometimes attended by circumstances exceedingly
ludicrous, arising out of the trifling facts which were
sufficient to throw a large portion of the community
into a condition of the wildest excitement and dismay.
In the July and August numbers of the "Wesleyan
Methodist Magazine" for 1863, more than two years
before the late tragedy in Jamaica occurred, there
appeared an account, by the present writer, of a wide-
spread panic in the parish where the late outbreak took
place, nearly leading to the proclamation of martial
law,—and all arising from the trifling incident of a
Methodist Society-ticket being found in the box of a
deceased slave by the plantation authorities, bearing the
printed inscription, "The kingdom of heaven suffereth
violence, and the violent take it by force." Too
ignorant to understand that this was only a verse of the
New Testament, which was printed on the ticket and
given to the possessor of it as a token of Church mem-

bership in the Methodist Society, the intelligent officials on the estate, and the astute magistrates, and other authorities of the parish, to whom the circumstance had been referred as wearing a most suspicious aspect, at once jumped to the conclusion that some fearful conspiracy was on foot to destroy the lives of the white inhabitants, of which this "seditious paper" furnished the "proof strong as holy writ." When it further came to light that the Methodist Missionary residing in the town had given out some hundreds of similar documents among the slaves in the neighbourhood, nothing could be more certain, in the estimation of these wise men, than that this most timely discovery of the dreadful plot had saved the island from all the terrible consequences of a slave rebellion. The militia were called out, and the parochial authorities assembled in all possible haste; scores, if not hundreds, of poor blacks, to their unutterable surprise, were captured. It was gravely proposed that the island should be proclaimed under martial law; and the wildest excitement and terror prevailed, until the Methodist preacher, who had been summoned before the civil and military authorities, assembled in solemn conclave, revealed the hitherto unsuspected truth, that "*the highly seditious words*" on the supposed treasonable documents were simply a quotation from St. Matthew's Gospel; (proof of which was given, after some delay in hunting up the fragment of a Bible used for swearing witnesses in the parochial courts;) and that the paper which had created such a profound sensation had been given in recognition of the fact that the deceased slave was a communicant in the Methodist Church. Thus fortunately the bubble burst before any serious evil had been done.

An incident equally insignificant constituted the principal, if not the only, basis upon which ex-Governor

Eyre rested the assertion that a terrible plot had been formed against the Government, and also involving in its objects the destruction of the white and coloured, as distinguished from the black, population; thereby throwing the whole country into a panic it has not yet recovered from, and such as could lead even tender-hearted women to palliate and excuse acts of cruelty and atrocity, against which under other circumstances their whole nature would have revolted. It is not one of the least of Mr. Eyre's misdoings that he palmed upon the community he was unfortunately appointed to govern, and as far as he could upon the British Government and upon the world, the most groundless slanders against the Negro population of Jamaica, and falsely charged upon them the intention to commit crimes which never had a place in their imagination, holding up to public reprobation as monsters of cruelty and crime a people as humane and well-disposed as any class of peasantry in Her Majesty's dominions.

When the Royal Commissioners had finished their arduous labours, after the most elaborate and searching investigation, they found no traces of the plot which Mr. Eyre and his coadjutors had conjured up to frighten themselves and the peaceful inhabitants of the island. It has since transpired that the trifling incident, exalted and magnified by fear into positive proof that a barbarous massacre of the white and coloured inhabitants was in contemplation, admits of a most simple and natural explanation. With many other bug-a-boo stories, put forth to alarm a too credulous people, it was stated that amongst the papers of Mr. G. W. Gordon, when examined by the authorities, there had been discovered a plan of Kingston, the principal city of the island, on which were marked the several places of rendezvous where the rebel blacks were to assemble for the purpose of capturing and burning the city and destroying the inhabitants. The terror produced by this statement was indescribable; and multitudes were afraid to go to bed at night, lest they should be massacred as they slept, or only awake to find burning and bloodshed all around them. This state of terror lasted for weeks, even after the so-called rebellion had been put down according to official announcement; it being far more easy to excite than to allay the fears of the people. And after all the stir made about the discovery of this famous paper, which was to prove G. W. Gordon a more wicked and sanguinary conspirator than Guy Fawkes himself, it turned out to be nothing more than the mischievous prank of an idle boy. Some years ago a youth, long since advanced to manhood, was employed in some inferior clerkship in G. W. Gordon's office or counting-house; and in an idle mood he one day amused himself with sketching from memory a rude plan of the city, (Kingston,) placing marks at certain places that possessed for unexplained reasons some sort of interest to himself. This was placed amongst other miscellaneous papers in his desk, and was forgotten. There it remained unnoticed for years, until the youth had passed into manhood and the time came when it pleased Governor Eyre to apprehend Mr. Gordon, and carry him to Morant Bay to be tried and put to death. His papers being then seized and examined, this boyish production came to light, and, without further investigation, was hastily pronounced by the sagacious helpers and advisers of Mr. Eyre to be indisputable proof of a conspiracy amongst the blacks, of which Mr. Gordon was the promoter and abettor, to massacre the white and coloured inhabitants, and burn the city. Thus it was that, scared by shadows from which no man of true courage and self-possession would have apprehended any danger, the local authorities terrified the people of Jamaica with the groundless fears which had taken possession of their own minds, to the exclusion of all that was manly and dignified, and sanctioned the atrocities that are so strongly denounced in the admirable charge of the Lord Chief Justice of England as offences against British law and humanity of no common degree.

The riot at Morant Bay was a sudden outburst of popular fury, unconnected with any plot, and confined to the parish and neighbourhood in which it originated; but resulting from a general feeling of discontent which had long been chronic among the black population. Its causes were both proximate and remote, reaching back to the time immediately succeeding the era of emancipation. Those who are acquainted with the history of events in Jamaica from 1834 will recognise in the Morant Bay riot one of the fruits of the mis-government and mal-administration by which the labouring classes had been oppressed from the time they were released from the shackles of slavery. The planting interest, so called, has always been dominant, infusing its own evil selfish spirit into the legislation of the colony, and controlling the administration of the laws for its own purposes, more especially in the inferior courts. By a persistent attempt, extending over more than thirty years, to engraft a new system of slavery upon the freedom which the philanthropy of the British nation had wrought out for the colonies, they engendered a spirit of mutual hostility between the proprietary and labouring classes, and produced a want of confidence which has been fatal to the interests of most of the Jamaica landholders, and brought their once splendid estates to ruin; while it has been disastrous to the civilization and well-being of the people them-

selves. In the legislature, the principal object of the
ruling party, never lost sight of, was to keep down the
emancipated classes, and so shape the laws enacted
from time to time that the great burden of taxation
should fall upon them, and as lightly as possible upon
their employers. The peasantry were even compelled
to pay a most unequal share of the enormous expense
incurred in several abortive schemes of immigration,
intended solely to lower and keep down, as near
starvation-point as possible, the wages they were to
receive for their labour. This suicidal policy was per-
sisted in, until the black labourers, systematically
oppressed and defrauded by the hirelings who were
chiefly intrusted with the charge of the plantations,
were driven in self-defence to purchase, and depend for
sustenance upon, their own small freeholds ; and thus a
vast number of valuable estates, which, under wise and
just management, would have continued to yield an ample
income to their absentee proprietors, were thrown out
of cultivation, and left to be overrun with bush.
Under such circumstances, it is no wonder that a spirit
of dissatisfaction spread widely amongst the people, and
they lost confidence both in their employers and in the
law-makers, highly appreciating the kind services of such
men as Mr. G. W. Gordon, who boldly stood forth to
expose and withstand the abuses by which the masses
of the people were wronged. The Rev. Henry Clarke,
island curate in the parish of Westmoreland, Jamaica,
says :—

" I have lived in this island during the last eighteen years,
and have never had but one opinion of its government,
which has been as corrupt, immoral, and oppressive, as any
which has ever existed on the face of the earth. The whole
influence of the Negro-hating, slavery-loving oligarchy which
has ruled us has been openly and avowedly directed to the

impoverishing of the Negroes, in order that they might be able to compel them to work at their own rate of wages. This was the object of high import duties on the necessaries of life, and of Coolie immigration; which, of my own knowledge, I affirm to be a most atrocious form of the slave-trade and of slavery, expressly designed to lower the wages of the free Negro.......I attribute the existing poverty and demoralization among the people of my district, in a great measure, to the practice which the estates adopted of moving the Negro villages periodically, in order to prevent the labourers from profiting by the bread-fruits, cocoa-nuts, and other trees of slow growth, which they plant around their dwellings. Every village of the estates in this district, of five thousand inhabitants, has been moved within the last ten years; and as the people have to pull down and rebuild their cottages at their own expense, they have got into the way of erecting miserable little huts, in which the poor things are compelled to live, like pigs in a sty. I now humbly thank God that I have not appealed to Him in vain, and that He has scattered, as in a moment, that detestable oligarchy which for full two hundred years has bought, sold, flogged, robbed, maimed, tortured, and debauched the poor black people of Jamaica. The licentiousness of white men in Jamaica has been, and in many parts is still, as boundless as it is unblushing. The laws, as well as the records, of Jamaica are such as should make every honest Englishman blush with shame for the savage barbarities his countrymen are capable of, when left to the exercise of their natural propensities, unrestrained by any fear of public opinion or of the law. The Negroes are as loyal and peaceable, and would be as industrious and virtuous, as any people in the world, if they were wisely and honestly governed. I would not be understood to mean that Negroes are better than English labourers would be under like circumstances; but they certainly are not worse. All men are alike bad: it is only early training and the grace of God which make the difference in any of us. Now that Her Majesty has assumed the government of this island, I believe that peace and prosperity will prevail in it. But the change must be complete to be effective; and there must be a complete sweep of Jamaica magistrates as well as of Jamaica legislators."

The Baptist Missionaries, in their statement presented to the Governor in 1865, make the following remarks :—

" Numbers of persons in various parts of the island are in a starving condition.......The greater number have the greatest possible difficulty to support themselves and their families.......Among the foregoing causes of poverty and distress, we have referred your Excéllency to the want of employment. In some districts, numbers of people are known to walk from six to thirty miles in search of work. Numbers, even in crop time, applying to the estates for employment, are turned back without obtaining it.......In all parts of the island a reduction of wages is expected, in most cases to the extent of from twenty-five to fifty per cent. ......On very few properties can land be leased for a term of years; and, consequently, the small grower cannot risk the cultivation of produce which stands more than twelve months. Coffee, which takes three years to come into bearing, he cannot plant; because he would have no hope of reaping the benefit. In most cases the tenant is subject to a six months' notice to quit; and, not unfrequently, no sooner has he planted off an acre, say of ground provisions, than such a notice is served upon him.......Not only have ground provisions increased in price, but there has been a great advance in the price of imported food; while the price of clothing used by the people has been doubled, and in some places even trebled.......The increase which has taken place has been greatly augmented by the Legislature allowing the *ad valorem* duty of twelve and a half per cent. to remain the same.......The effect of placing heavy duties upon the food and clothing of the labouring classes has been to check improvement.......In many districts Creole labour has been displaced wholly or in part by that of Coolies, Chinese, and Africans.......The cost of these immigration schemes to the country your Excellency will find to have been enormous.   We believe an examination of the official returns will show that, from 1834 to the present time, it has not been much less than four hundred thousand pounds.......Complaints are made on account of the marked distinction, to the prejudice of the small settler, in favour of the great proprietor.   The small settler has to pay for his horse or mule eleven shillings, and for his ass three shillings and sixpence; while the working stock on the estates—steers, mules, and horned kind—are taxed only sixpence per head.......The peasantry suffer great hardships from the tardy administration of justice in some of our petty courts."

To the evils of partial and corrupt legislation were added those of partial and corrupt administration in the inferior local courts, amounting in many instances to a practical denial of justice.   The planters themselves were largely intrusted with magisterial commissions, which enabled them to play into each other's hands in most cases involving questions between the employer and the employed, and cut off the weaker party from the redress which oft-inflicted wrong demanded.   Questions of alleged damage by stray cattle, and of wages detained on various pretexts by the planters, afforded frequent opportunities of mutual obligation and accommodation, on the principle of "Claw me, claw thee," between those who were most improperly intrusted with the administration of the laws.   This evil prevailed to a fearful extent in St. Thomas-in-the-East, the scene of the late outbreak, where a faction, of which the rector and some members of his family were the head, ran riot in oppression and injustice of this kind. Nor was it confined to the locality that has been mentioned. Mr. Justice Ker, one of the judges of Jamaica, says :—

"I am called upon to observe, however, that St. Ann's has long had a real grievance. That grievance is the fact, that the confidential clerk and manager of the leading mercantile firm there, the Messrs. Bravo, is at the same time clerk of the magistrates and deputy clerk of the peace. It is utterly impossible but that a very large proportion of the cases which come before the magistrates for adjudication are cases in which the Messrs. Bravo are either directly or indirectly interested, or in which they have, or are believed to have, a bias. But could an uninstructed population ever be persuaded that justice would be done in such cases? In point of fact, they do not believe it, as I have occasion very well to know. The influence exercised by the clerk of the magistrates over the Bench is necessarily very great, sometimes paramount. Some recent decisions from St. Ann's, which have been brought to my notice, have given me a most unfavourable impression of the administration of justice in that parish."

The following petition, presented to Governor Eyre a short time before the outbreak, and signed chiefly by those who afterwards perished in the bloody retribution exacted by Mr. Eyre and his advisers, will show how largely the abuses prevailing in the local courts of justice contributed to promote the prevalent feeling of discontent that led to the sad outburst of popular fury at Morant Bay :—

"We most humbly beg to implore Your Majesty's attention to our humble communications. When we were slaves, we never had such heavy work; and after having finished those number of chains, with the expectation, at the end of the week, to obtain the amount of six shillings, we generally get one shilling and sixpence to two shillings and sixpence for the whole week's pay. The island has been ruined consequently of the advantage that is taken of us by the managers of estates. Whenever we have a case which may be taken before the planter magistrates, they give us no satisfaction whatever, but combines with each other and takes away our rights. We most humbly beseech Your Majesty, that it may please Your Majesty to appoint a stipendiary magistrate to sit at every court day, as may enable us to obtain satisfaction. All we ask is, that Your Majesty may be pleased to consider over the state of this island, and render the poor some assistance; and that Your Majesty's life may be long spared, and that the blessings of those ready to perish may rest upon you.

"ANDREW ROSS,"
and thirty-nine others.

"*St. Thomas-in-the-East,*
        "*September 5th*, 1865."

This petition, signed only five weeks before the outbreak, and placed in the hands of Mr. Eyre for transmission to Her Majesty, sheds light upon the causes of the riot, and serves to make manifest how painfully the people were feeling the oppressions heaped upon them by partial and class legislation, and unjust interested magistrates, when those events occurred which immediately produced the catastrophe.

But one of the most crying evils under which Jamaica has groaned, is the incubus of a costly Established Church, which on the whole has done far more to hinder than to promote the advancement of religion and civilization in the colony. Until the labours of Moravian and Wesleyan Missionaries awakened religious feelings amongst the black and coloured population, and, through their agency, Churches were raised up and established amongst these despised and neglected masses; the clergy, supported in connexion with the

State in the several parishes, regarded the free coloured
people and slaves as forming no part whatever of their
spiritual and pastoral charge, and gave no more attention to them than they did to the cattle on the plantations.   Then, influenced less by concern for the interests of immortal souls than by sectarian intolerance, they
began, for the first time, to devote to these contemned
classes some degree of attention, and to admit them,
very sparingly and ungraciously, to Church privileges;
and as the Missionaries, by their earnest and zealous
labours, spread religious knowledge with its benign
influences in various localities, breaking up the fallow
ground which none others thought of cultivating,
Episcopal agents uniformly stepped in, and Episcopal
churches were erected to absorb the fruit of missionary
effort; all this being done at the public expense, and
the Nonconformists themselves subjected to taxation,
for the purpose of robbing them of the legitimate results of their self-denying toil.   In this way Episcopalian
churches (founded, in most cases, upon the results of
missionary labour) were multiplied, until they over-
spread the land, furnishing lucrative situations for many
of the sons and friends of the more influential Creole
families, until the public burthens for State Church
purposes were increased to the amount of some forty-five
thousand pounds *per annum*, absorbing a large portion
of the revenue of the island.   The wrong done to the
Wesleyan and Baptist Churches especially, by this system
of oppression, was very great.   The membership of both
these denominations was considerably in advance of that
pertaining to the State Church; yet all were compelled
alike to contribute to the taxation levied for the purpose
of building Episcopalian places of worship, and paying
the stipends of ministers, for the advantage of the more
wealthy portion of the community; and then, unaided

by the revenues they were compelled to raise, they had to make similar provision for themselves. To aggravate the evil, the men, thus sustained by funds largely extorted from other religious communities, were very frequently possessed of none of the more important qualifications required for the office they filled; and, in too many instances, their lives were a reproach to the religion of which they professed to be the ministers. Nor is this evil yet removed. It is no violation of Christian charity,—for it is no violation of truth,—to say that a great proportion of the State clergy, whose support is largely derived, to the present day, from the taxation of Missionary and non-Episcopal churches in the West Indies, have no moral fitness for the office. But for this system of monstrous injustice, absorbing and neutralizing the effects of Missionary labour, the moral and religious condition of the British West Indian colonies would have been far in advance of what it now is. Whatever may be said concerning State-churchism in the mother country, nearly forty years' observation and experience in various colonies has fully satisfied me that in the West Indies it has been the reverse of a blessing, and has produced a far greater amount of evil than of good. Recent events show that it has been a principal element of evil in Jamaica, and contributed in no small degree to augment the dissatisfaction prevailing amongst the labouring classes; especially when men, interested in the welfare of the masses, like William Knibb and George William Gordon, called attention to the manner in which the entire population, of all denominations, were, upon the principle that "*might is right*," compelled, whether they were willing or not, to give a portion of their hard earnings to provide religious advantages for the wealthier few. It

c

required clearer vision than large numbers of the
people possessed to discover any shade of moral distinction between such a system of legalized plunder
and highway robbery. In both cases it amounts to—
" You must give us your property for our advantage ;
and if not, we will take it by force."

CHAPTER II.

THE operation of these and other similar causes produced that state of general dissatisfaction which became
so strikingly manifest when the letter of Dr. Underhill, the Secretary of the Baptist Missionary Society,
addressed to Mr. Cardwell, the Colonial Secretary, was
made public; and large meetings, in all parts of the
island, endorsed the complaints embodied in that letter
concerning the grievances under which the industrial
classes were groaning. But nowhere was this dissatisfaction more strongly cherished than amongst the large
population of St. Thomas-in-the-East, where local
oppression and abuse of authority extensively prevailed.
Partiality and injustice reigned in the local courts, in
which planter influence predominated, until the people
had lost all hope of obtaining redress of any
grievance; for every magistrate who endeavoured
to exercise fair dealing, and hold the scales of
justice evenly, was sure to be shuffled out of office
on some pretence or other, or removed elsewhere,
through the corrupt influences that had gained ascend-
ancy in the parish. These were of such a nature as
strikingly to illustrate the malign power of the Church
establishment, and the gross oppression to which the
people were subjected. The rector of the parish was
one of the old-time, slave-holding clergymen, two of
his sons filling public offices in the same parish; so
that this family with its connexions gave whatever
direction they pleased to parochial affairs: and the
vestry, which this family largely controlled, possessing

the power to impose parochial taxes, (including the
demands made for various ecclesiastical purposes,) the
Nonconformist congregations, which included a great
majority of the people, were subjected to unjust bur-
dens that were very keenly felt.   The Custos—for so
the principal magistrate in the parish is designated,
holding a position somewhat analogous to the Lord-
Lieutenancy of an English county—was the unfortunate Baron Von Ketelholdt, who was among the
earliest victims of the outbreak; and he was a man
possessing but little strength of character, so that he
was easily moulded to the purposes of the ruling faction,
—a weakness which ultimately cost him his life.
Large amounts had been levied, during several years
past, by local taxation upon the people, to build a
church in one of the parochial districts, where a new
church was not truly required; for the character of the
resident clergyman was so much at a discount that
few cared to attend his ministry; and this church-
building scheme was well known in the neighbourhood
to be only a gross piece of jobbery, designed not so
much to serve the public good as to put a large sum of
money into the pocket of the clergyman himself,—the
Rev. Mr. Herschell,—who was also among the early
victims of the riot, and who, contrary to all precedent
and all propriety, was suffered to become the contractor
for the erection of this ecclesiastical structure.   And
his conduct in connexion therewith was such as to
create much offence, and bring obloquy upon his name,
which even the tragical circumstances of his death have
not been sufficient to obliterate.   Another extensive
ecclesiastical structure, still standing in an unfinished
state near to the scene of the outbreak at Morant Bay,
was also commenced, at a heavy expense to the people
of the parish; though the vast majority of them had no

manner of interest in these buildings, which, if erected at all, should have been at the cost of those—the more wealthy class—for whose immediate benefit or convenience they were intended.

Under these complicated oppressions, aggravated by drought and poverty, the labouring people groaned in St. Thomas-in-the-East; and when George William Gordon, whose tragic fate has called forth such widespread sympathy and indignation, interposed to obtain redress of existing grievances, he, at the instigation of the corrupt clique ruling over the parish, was treated by Governor Eyre with gross injustice, the sanctioning of which reflects but little honour upon the Duke of Newcastle, the Colonial Secretary of that day, and stands in unfavourable contrast with the proceedings of the Colonial Office when men like Sir George Murray, or Lord Goderich, were in power there. Mr. Gordon, like other men, doubtless had his infirmities; and perhaps it may be true that, if he had been somewhat less impulsive and impetuous, he might have accomplished a larger amount of good; but there is no reason to believe that he was otherwise than a good and sincere man, advocating, from disinterested motives, the rights of a down-trodden people, and labouring with earnest zeal to obtain redress of the numerous wrongs to which he saw them subjected. As one of the landed proprietors of St. Thomas-in-the-East, and representing the parish in the colonial parliament with no mean ability, his influence was powerfully felt in the parish vestry, in opposition to the selfish faction dominant there; while he also stood forth as the stern uncompromising opponent of those measures which he deemed to be corrupt and oppressive in connexion with the administration of Governor Eyre.

To persons who are not acquainted with the real

merits of the case it may appear that, if Gordon was somewhat harshly treated, he deserved in great measure what was done to him, as a factious and interested demagogue, taking advantage of the ignorance of the masses to stir them up against lawful authority, and render them dissatisfied with their condition and their rulers. Nothing has been wanting on the part of Mr. Eyre and his adherents, to give this complexion to the case, and traduce the character of the murdered man : but a true insight into the facts warrants a widely different view, and shows that Gordon made himself enemies by his fidelity in exposing and rebuking real abuses both in parochial affairs and in the general government of the Colony, and at length became the innocent victim of political rancour, persecuted to death by as gross an abuse of trust, and as violent an outrage against law and justice, as the records of British Colonial history will furnish.

George William Gordon was born in slavery. He was the son of Mr. Joseph Gordon, who was a planting attorney on a large scale, having the oversight of a considerable number of plantations by power of attorney from the absentee proprietors, from which he derived an ample income. He was Custos of St. Andrew, the parish in which he resided ; and he also represented the parish in the House of Assembly. The mother of G. W. Gordon was a slave ; and, according to rule in such cases, the child followed the condition of the mother. But, by the profitable exercise of the intelligence and energy with which he was gifted, he acquired sufficient means to purchase his freedom and that of his slave-born sisters ; and when, as the result of the changes brought about by the abolition of slavery, the once wealthy father became involved in pecuniary embarrassments, the son, born to an inheritance of shame and servitude, nobly stepped forward to his help, and purchased the property of the father, to leave him in possession of it and in the enjoyment of the earthly comforts to which he had been accustomed. At the same time he won his way to a position of respectability and influence, as a member of the Legislature and a proprietor of the soil. These unchallenged facts show that George William Gordon was, both intellectually and morally, a man of superior character. And the testimony of competent and highly respectable witnesses fully sustains this estimate of that deeply injured man.

The Rev. Dr. King, of the Church of Scotland, who knew him well, says :—

"Without pronouncing any judgment on recent occurrences, I am free to say that nothing but a total transformation of disposition, or unsettlement of reason, could involve such a man as he was in seditious schemes or bloody adventures. He was a member of a United Presbyterian Church in Kingston, of which I filled temporarily the pulpit. He aided and cheered me in the fulfilment of my duties. I stayed with him occasionally, and we had excursions together. I had every facility for knowing what was thought of him by judges, magistrates, clergymen, and society in general; and at that time every one, from the highest to the lowest, spoke of him with esteem. Mr. William Wemyss Anderson was one of the first who called my attention specially to him, by characterising him as a man of princely generosity and of unbounded benevolence."

Dr. Fiddes, a physician who stands at the head of his profession in Jamaica, and who knew Mr. Gordon from his youth, says :—

"I had been well acquainted with Gordon during the last twenty years; and, although I always regarded him as rather eccentric in his views and notions of the people's rights, and somewhat peculiar in his religious observances, I had nevertheless great respect for the power of his intellect and the innate force of his character. He was, moreover, a man of generous disposition, and possessed much kindness of heart. That he wished well to his country and countrymen, I am thoroughly convinced; that he ever counselled the people to the commission of acts of violence and murder, I do not believe."

"Mr. Gordon was personally known to me," says a member of the late Jamaica House of Assembly; "and Jamaica had a worthy and faithful son in him. It was impossible for him to escape the dangers which beset him, when he constantly proclaimed the wrongs done to the oppressed classes. I can bear witness to his faithful advocacy of the people's rights. I wish the Colony had fifty such men."

"Few," says another witness who knew him well, "are willing to confront the wrong doings of men who hold a position of public and important trust. This, Mr. Gordon dared to do; and for this, I believe, he has been called to suffer. To the maliciousness which seems to have prompted some of Mr. Gordon's foes, there appears to be no bounds. I speak from personal knowledge of Mr. Gordon, when I state that a more kind-hearted, humane, and generous man was not to be found in that Colony. Whenever an object of distress presented itself, none was more liberal in administering relief, none felt more deeply for the woes of suffering humanity, or was more prompt in mitigating that suffering. When we couple these things with the fact that Mr. Gordon was one of the largest land proprietors in Jamaica, nothing, I think, shows more clearly the improbability of his being the instigator of the late outbreak."

Such was the man whom Governor Eyre seized upon, bearing him away from the bosom of his family to the scene of merciless slaughter, as an eagle bears its prey in its clutch; and, without one emotion of relenting or pity, handed him over to those amiable rivals of Calcraft, Messrs. Nelson and Brand, to be immolated upon the altar of political strife. A few facts may suffice to explain the rancour of the faction ruling the affairs of the parish against Mr. Gordon, and the envenomed feelings so manifest in the proceedings of Mr. Eyre towards this injured man.

The rector of St. Thomas-in-the-East, already referred to, being solicited for alms by a diseased wanderer, took the extraordinary course of sending the poor man to the lock-up: an act which he had no authority to perform, as he was not a magistrate. The wretched outcast, thus sent to a place used only for punishment, and having no better shelter assigned to him than the privy of the establishment in a most disgusting state of filthiness, died there, with no hand to aid him in his last moments, and was then buried, contrary to law, without an inquest being held. This outrage against humanity and justice Mr. G. W. Gordon—who was a member of the vestry, a magistrate, and the representative of the parish in the Legislative Assembly—brought under the notice of the Governor, calling in question the conduct of the rector, and requesting an investigation. Contrary to all propriety, the matter was referred for inquiry to the parochial authorities, who were themselves also implicated in suffering such a state of things to exist in the parish as this case disclosed, instead of being placed, as it should have been, in the hands of a commission composed of disinterested men. The result was what might have been expected, and doubtless what Governor Eyre desired. All fair inquiry was smothered, and the inhuman and illegal conduct of the rector, in sending a man to prison on account of his poverty, was represented as a sort of imitation of the Good Samaritan. It was made, in the report of the magistrates, to bear the aspect of a deed of *charity;* and the poor outcast, according to them, was sent to the gaol for shelter, and to be taken care of! What kind of shelter was given to him, and what degree of care was exercised towards this poor human brother of the rector, may be inferred from the fact that he was found dead, after the lapse of a few days, in such a horrible place as the unventilated privy of a prison, where, during the whole time of his unlawful imprisonment, he had sat, and eaten, and drunk, and slept, until he slept the sleep of death. Surely, if this imitator of the Good Samaritan had wished to exercise the charity towards a suffering fellow-creature for which he would claim credit in this case, the spacious premises of the Morant Bay rectory, with its many out-rooms, might have furnished a less repulsive place of shelter; and the rector's ample income, derived from the public purse, might have furnished a little plain food to relieve his necessities, instead of turning him over to the cruel fate which befell him. A wondrous exercise of Christian charity, truly, to send a sick person to a gaol, to be fed, not at his own, but at the parochial expense!

The specious pretext was allowed to pass, and Mr. Gordon was censured for having called in question the humanity of the rector; and, further to throw dust in the eyes of the public, Mr. Gordon was also deprived by Governor Eyre of the commissions he held as a magistrate of several parishes. Strange to say, he failed to obtain redress of this grievance at the Colonial Office, although the Colonial Secretary, the Duke of Newcastle, censured both Mr. Eyre and the magistrates for their conduct in connexion with this inquiry in the following severe language: "I am unable to concur with you," says his grace, in a despatch addressed to Governor Eyre, " in the views which you have taken of the proceed-

ings of the justices ; nor can I regard the recapitulation
.contained in your despatch No. 52 as an accurate and
complete statement of the facts disclosed in the evidence......On the evidence of the gaoler there can be no
doubt that the gross and disgraceful abuses charged by
Mr. Gordon against the 'lock-up' house did exist in it
up to the time when it was visited by Mr. Gordon......
When the justices, finding the 'lock-up' house in this
state, then simply resolved that it was a very good one,
without the slightest notice of the scandalous abuses
which had been proved against it, they evaded the
whole question ; and when they refused to hear eleven
out of fourteen witnesses tendered by Mr. Gordon, on
the ground that the evidence proffered related not to
the then, but to the past, state of the 'lock-up' house,
they betrayed their duty."

There can be no doubt that this oppression of Mr.
Gordon, because of his attempt to redress the grievances which the case of this poor man disclosed, gave
intensity to the feeling of dissatisfaction already widely
prevailing in the parish, and tended further to destroy all
confidence in the integrity both of the parochial authorities and of the island government. And there can be
as little doubt that this effort of Mr. Gordon to correct
the abuses existing in the parish—rendered abortive to
a great extent by partiality and injustice—awakened
towards him that bitter hostility on the part of the
dominant faction in the parish and of Governor Eyre,
that culminated in his murder. Neither the one nor the
other could readily forgive the man who had brought
upon them such severe condemnation from the Colonial
Office, and exposed them to so public a humiliation.

Mr. Gordon aggravated the unkindly feeling with
which the Governor regarded him by the course he took as
a member of the local parliament in opposing official cor-

ruption and peculation. A notorious fraud had been perpetrated, well known as "*the tramway swindle,*" whereby
the public revenue which the people were heavily taxed
to sustain was defrauded of many thousand pounds.
Gross negligence and unfaithfulness on the part of Mr.
Eyre, as the head of the government, were alleged in
connexion with this business, and he was subjected to
heavy censure from many quarters, especially from the
Hon. George Price, a leading member of the local
government, who, in a large and well-written pamphlet, exposed, with scathing rebuke, the culpability
of the Governor, and the indifference of the Colonial
Office to the misconduct of its nominees in office. But
from none did Mr. Eyre experience more caustic condemnation than from Mr. Gordon, who, in his place as
a legislator, inveighed loudly against the corruption
which laid the people open to be plundered of their hard
earnings by greedy and dishonest officials. This was
not all. A grant of £1000 had been voted by the Legislature for sundry repairs to be done to the official residence of the Governor. In violation of all propriety, a
considerable part, some say £200, of this amount was
used for the purchase of a piano, which would of course
be more for the Governor's family use than the public
service, and, whenever he should remove from the
government, would very likely be included and sold in
the catalogue of his personal effects. This misappro-
priation of funds, voted for a different purpose, was
exposed and commented upon in the Legislature by Mr.
Gordon, and the amount had to be refunded. It is not
difficult to conceive how a circumstance of this kind,
more than anything else, would add intensity to the
bitterness of those feelings with which the Governor
regarded Mr. Gordon; and it sheds a gloomy light upon
the proceedings of the Jamaica authorities in con-

nection with the arrest and condemnation of that unfortunate gentleman.

A further mortification was brought upon the Governor, through Mr. Gordon's instrumentality, in the successful opposition he gave to sundry favourite measures recommended by Mr. Eyre to the colonial legislature. Amongst these were the construction of a dock at Kingston, which he opposed on the ground that it was unconstitutional to tax the whole of the people for what was really a private and speculative enterprise, and for the sole advantage of a small mercantile portion of the community. There were also bills passed on the Governor's recommendation to authorize capital punishment for petty offences, and to re-establish a district prison at Port Maria in a most unwholesome locality, and providing that hard labour should include the treadmill, shot drill, and crank. These Mr. Gordon resisted, as involving a return to the abolished barbarities of past evil times. Unable to resist the influence in the local legislature which the Governor was able to exert there to carry these objectionable measures through, Mr. Gordon exposed and protested against their evil tendency in a well-written letter to the Colonial Secretary, and succeeded in obtaining their disallowance by the Crown; thereby, doubtless, exasperating in no small degree the dislike with which he was regarded by the Governor and the servile men who served his purposes in the two legislative bodies.*

* The following are extracts from Mr. Gordon's letter to the Colonial Secretary:—

"Sir,—I have to bring before your notice, on behalf of the people of this country, the following facts, which are submitted as grievances. From gross mismanagement and for wasteful purposes, the taxation of the country is increased......The tramroad affair, besides having involved the country in a heavy expenditure, has also, by interfering with the principal public road, caused serious loss of stock to the passengers. The Governor, in his

Next came the celebrated Underhill letter, to which Mr. Eyre attached so much importance as causing the outbreak, forgetting that he himself was solely responsible for the agitation it produced in the island, inasmuch as it was he who gave it all the publicity it acquired. This letter, containing a temperate and able statement of the grievances under which the labouring classes of Jamaica were ground to the earth, was addressed to the Colonial Minister, Mr. Cardwell, who referred it in an official despatch to Mr. Eyre, for him to report upon it. With unpardonable indiscretion, if he really

opening speech, recommends a project of a dock, which certainly is not one for which the people should be taxed. Is it constitutional to tax the people for speculative enterprises? This is a measure which, if allowed to take effect, will create new heart-burnings in the minds of the inhabitants generally, and is a great public wrong.

"A Bill was passed to inflict corporal punishment for petty offences...... This measure is strictly one aimed against the lower classes, who just now are in a state of great destitution. If you could only behold them, your feelings of compassion would be aroused to mercy and relief, instead of the inflic- tion of corporal punishment, which is death, or next to it. Representations, unfounded and uncharitable, may be wickedly made against the peasants of this country; but, in good truth, they are as peaceable, civil, and well- disposed, as any people can well be. What they require is, what has been neglected,—attention to their sanitary improvement, and relief, to some extent, from the excessive taxation on the necessary articles of food and clothing. These are the points which are lost sight of for the debasing purposes of the whip.

"A Bill was also passed to re-establish a district prison at Port Maria, which provides that hard labour shall include the hand-mill, shot-drill, and crank. Port Maria is the grave of Jamaica. Yet the prison, which was abolished, is again to be re-established, with the iron shackles; to which the unfortunate prisoners have been consigned by the present Governor, with hard labour. From the depreciated state of health to which the prisoners must be reduced at Port Maria, many of them will leave the prison to be for ever after worthless, and a tax upon society. When it is remembered that many are sent to prison for minor offences—in many cases wrongfully, and under wrong sentences—by erring judgments and unlearned justices, it does seem that it is a most cruel proceeding. I only write from the stern obligations of a sense of justice and common humanity."

believed in the wide-spread disaffection reported by him to exist amongst the people, Mr. Eyre took measures which caused Dr. Underhill's letter to be circulated in every newspaper printed in the colony, calling forth an almost universal response of such a character as indicated how general was the dissatisfaction among all classes of the community with the state of affairs and the government of the island. At the public meetings, held in the several parishes, Mr. Gordon took a prominent part in exposing existing abuses, and thus further incurred the enmity of the Governor, who appears to have been rendered furious by the opposition to his own grovelling, short-sighted policy which these meetings developed. This was evident from the significant fact, that when martial law was proclaimed, a large number, besides the unfortunate Gordon, who had taken part in these public meetings, were pounced upon by Governor Eyre and his agents and made prisoners, being sent to Morant Bay, and delivered over to the tender mercies of Nelson and Ramsay, under the impudent pretext that they wer parties to the Morant Bay outbreak, and concerned in the imaginary plot which the Governor's own cowardice had conjured up; as if it were probable that planters, legal and medical practitioners, editors of newspapers, and members of the Legislature, all of them white men, or so nearly approaching it as to be married into respectable white families, and all of them in easy, if not affluent, circumstances, would enter into a conspiracy with the Negroes to assassinate all the white and coloured inhabitants,—including, of course, by inference, themselves and their own families,—that the blacks might possess the island for themselves. A more palpable absurdity could scarcely have been conceived. It is remarkable that the whole of those men who were

arrested by command of Governor Eyre, and ignomini-
ously hurried off to Morant Bay, to be tried like
Gordon by court-martial, were parties who had taken a
prominent share in the Underhill meetings, so called.
It was no relenting on the part of Mr. Eyre that saved
these innocent men from sharing the fate of Gordon;
but the misgivings which arose, rather tardily, in the
minds of some of the principal military authorities as
to the legality of trying and executing civilians by
military tribunals, for alleged political offences committed by them long anterior to the existence of martial
law; a procedure which the charge of the Lord Chief
Justice of England stigmatizes with the guilt of murder,
inasmuch as it is putting men to death without any
authority of law.

CHAPTER III.

THE preceding observations serve to explain what had been for a long time the condition of affairs, and what was the state of public feeling in the island, when, on Saturday, the 7th of October, two planter justices of the peace—Mr. Walton, the owner of a plantation in the vicinity, who was among the slain of the following week, and another—were sitting in the Morant Bay court-house, adjudicating cases which planters ought not to have been competent judicially to meddle with, inasmuch as they involved questions of land occupation, and other matters upon which planters were not likely to give a fair and unbiassed judgment; it being well understood that planter magistrates would help and favour each other, and hold on to planter interests in all questions at issue between the labourers and their employers. For some cause never explained, the decisions of the two Magistrates on this occasion failed to give satisfaction to the black people, who filled the court-house in considerable numbers; and they expressed their discontent, according to their wont, in audible murmurs. This gave offence to the magisterial dignitaries, who ordered that the murmurers should be taken into custody by the police. On hearing this order given, the people immediately retired from the court-house; and outside the officers attempted to arrest one of the number, whom they had marked as signifying dissatisfaction with the proceedings of the magistrates. This act was alike illegal and unwise, as the police had no authority without a warrant to arrest men out of the

D

court, and the evil complained of had ceased as soon as notice was taken of it.   It was resisted by the man's friends; and the attempt proved abortive, having no other result than to increase the indignation of the people, already smarting under grievous wrongs.   If the magistrates had exercised the forbearance which any English judge would have shown, and let the matter rest here, they would have acted discreetly; but on the following Monday, when the court resumed its sittings, a black man named Paul Bogle, (who from his superior intelligence exerted considerable influence amongst the labourers in the neighbourhood in which he lived,) when the Magistrates, in an alleged case of trespass, sentenced a person to fine or imprisonment, interposed his advice to the man, as he had a perfect right to do, to give notice that he would appeal against the Magistrates' decision.   Irritated by Bogle's interference, the Magistrates, yielding to spiteful feeling, very foolishly fell back upon and revived the old case, and proceeded to issue warrants against Bogle and several others on the charge of interfering with the police in the execution of their duty.   This amounted to something like a declaration of war against the black people concerned, who had certainly done nothing more than resist, very unwisely perhaps, the illegal apprehension of a man without a warrant ; and it could scarcely have any other effect, considering the provocation already given, than to stir them up to resist violence with violence.

The next day a posse of officers, ludicrously small, (as it consisted of only three or four men,) was sent to apprehend the offenders, amounting to some twenty-eight, whose names were included in the warrants Wrought up by this time to something approaching desperation, Bogle and his associates resisted the officers, and made them prisoners; dismissing them, however, after a short time, without harm or insult. Thus the magistrates went blundering on, and by their reckless intemperate proceedings raised a spirit which they could neither subdue nor control.

On Wednesday, the 11th of October, the quarterly meeting of the parish Vestry was to be held; and the parish authorities, with the Custos at their head, alarmed at the demonstrations of the last few days, and without sufficient discretion to remonstrate with the excited and misguided people, and endeavour to bring them to reason by mild and conciliatory measures, could think of nothing but a resort to brute force. Accordingly a despatch was sent off to the Governor, giving an exaggerated account of what had occurred, and calling for military aid. Meanwhile, a small body of volunteers belonging to the parish was summoned to Morant Bay, to afford protection to the Vestry, because it was rumoured that Paul Bogle, and a large number of the people with him, intended that day to go down to the Bay. A more unfortunate step could not have been taken; and to this foolish act of calling out the volunteers may be attributed all the deplorable results which ensued. Even as it was, if there had been amongst the authorities one person gifted with cool self-possession and sound discretion, to go out and advise the people to abstain from violence, there would have been no outbreak, and the fatal collision of that day would have been prevented. It was an unfortunate circumstance that Mr. Gordon was, through indisposition, prevented from attending that vestry meeting, of which he was a member; for, no doubt, had he been present, he would have pointed out to the people that they were acting unadvisedly, and taking an unwise course to obtain redress of their grievances: and a few words from him, whom they knew and respected, would have been sufficient. But he was not there, through illness; and there was not one present, either clergyman, magistrate, or vestryman, that had the courage and good sense to do what the emergency and humanity demanded.

The meeting of the Vestry took place, and the business proceeded to its close without any interruption. The members of the Vestry were about to regale themselves with the dinner usually provided on such occasions, at the expense of the parish; but before the viands, which were in course of preparation, could be served, a large assembly of people made their appearance at the entrance of the square in which the court-house stood. It has never been explained what specific purpose they had in view, in marching into the town as they did; but it was probably nothing more than was meant by the late Reform gatherings in London, which were designed for no purposes of violence, but as demonstrations, on the part of those who took part in them, to assert what they conceived to be their claims to right and justice. The elaborate investigations of the Royal Commission, directed especially to this point, failed to elicit the slightest evidence that any plot existed amongst the Negroes. They brought no fire-arms with them; for those which they afterwards used they took from the police station, after they found the volunteers drawn up in hostile array to receive them; and the fact that those who were killed after the attack upon the court-house were in most, if not all cases, beaten to death, and not hewn down, would show that they had not even armed themselves with the cutlass, a large knife, used as the chief implement of their daily toil. The conclusion to which we are brought by a fair consideration of all that has come to light is, that the assembling of the mob, upon the 11th of October, was an unpremeditated and ill-judged act, consequent upon the injudicious and culpable proceedings of the local authorities. The brutal and indiscriminate massacre of all who were connected with, or present at, the riot, who could have shed light upon the subject, has rendered it impossible that any satisfactory information can be obtained as to the views and purposes of the rioters; but the facts, that no traces of any plot or organization could be discovered; that they proceeded to Morant Bay, unarmed; that they did not injure, or attempt to injure, any individual, until they were fired upon, and a considerable number of them killed or wounded,—render it absurd to look upon the movement as an attempt at rebellion, or anything more than a sudden riot, capable of being altogether prevented by the exercise of something like discretion on the part of the unfortunate men in the court-house, who paid with their lives the penalty of those errors into which their fears hurried them.

This is fully borne out by the petition which was addressed to the Governor only the day before the riot took place, signed by James Dacres, Paul Bogle, James M'Laren, and others, who were afterwards hurried to the gallows by military tribunals. In this remarkable document they complain of the conduct of the Magistrates; represent themselves as loyal to the Queen; express their belief that the attack made upon them by the police at Morant Bay (on the preceding Saturday) was an outrageous assault, and that they had the right to resist the arrest of innocent persons. They further complain of wrongs spreading over the past twenty-seven years, and call upon the Governor to protect them from the oppressions they were subject to; and intimate that if he will not do so, they will be compelled to put their own shoulders to the wheel, with due obeisance to the laws of the Queen and country. The following is the petition of these oppressed villagers :—

"We, the petitioners of St. Thomas-in-the-East, do send to inform Your Excellency of the mean advantages that has been taken of us from time to time; and more especially this present time, when, on Saturday, the 7th of this month, an outrageous assault was committed on us by the policemen of this parish, by order of the justices, which occasioned an outbreaking; for which warrants have been issued against innocent persons, which we were compelled to resist. We therefore call upon Your Excellency for protection, seeing we are Her Majesty's loyal subjects ; which protection, if refused, we will be compelled to put our shoulders to the wheels, as we have been imposed upon for a period of twenty-seven years, with due obeisance to the laws of our Queen and country, and we can no longer endure the same.

"Therefore is our object of calling upon Your Excellency ; and your petitioners, as in duty bound, will ever pray.

"James Dacres,
Paul Bogle,
James M'Laren, and others."

This certainly is not the language of those who were engaged in, and about to carry into effect, a deadly conspiracy against the Government, and to destroy the white and coloured people ; but that of men honestly appealing to the right quarter for the redress of crying grievances; and is, in itself, sufficient proof that the riot which took place on the following day must have been unpremeditated, provoked by circumstances which occurred immediately after the petition had been forwarded to the Governor.

The conduct of Mr. Eyre with regard to this important paper was most extraordinary and reprehensible; and serves to show his utter want of candour, and the little reliance that is to be placed upon his representations of the outbreak, and the causes which produced it. This petition was sent by a special messenger; and it is in evidence that it was placed in the Governor's hands on the forenoon of the 11th, a very short time after he had received the communication of the Custos, requesting military aid. Had he been a wise and prudent man, and equal to the duties of his position, he would have acted as his predecessor in office, Earl Mulgrave, did on a somewhat similar occasion. Repairing without delay to the spot where mischief was evidently threatening, and acquainting himself with the real merits of the case, he would have addressed himself to the application of the remedy required. But, strange to say, with an indifference which shows in a striking point of view his unfitness for the position he occupied, he simply gave orders for a military force to be sent, suppressed the petition of the complaining Negroes, and betook himself to a dinner-party in the mountains. And, after the collision had taken place which these two communications showed to be imminent, he altogether put away the important petition of the oppressed people which had been conveyed to him, making no mention of it in his official dispatches to the Colonial Office. It would probably never have been brought forward, important as it is in throwing light upon the events of those few memorable days and the real purposes of the unfortunate Negroes, had he not been compelled to produce it through questions put to him by the counsel employed by the Jamaica Committee to watch the proceedings of the Royal Commission.

But yet more strange is the fact that the poor fellow who carried the petition to the Governor was punished with a severe flogging by the notorious Ramsay, whether with the connivance and sanction of Mr. Eyre does not very clearly appear; but it is difficult to imagine how, without such connivance, Ramsay could have become aware of the circumstances. And, as far as can be ascertained, every person who signed that petition, or was privy to it in any way, was mercilessly hunted down and put to death.

The unhappy events which occurred on the 11th of October are matters of sufficient notoriety. That the conduct of the complaining Negroes, in marching as they did to Morant Bay on the day of the vestry-meeting, was unwise and culpable, is not to be denied; but, even then, no such sad results as followed would have ensued, but for the much more culpable proceedings of the Custos, and those who were assembled with him in the court-house. Terrified beyond all reason and propriety, it seems never to have occurred to them that, before resorting to extremities, some one ought to go out and remonstrate with the advancing crowd, and advise them to return quietly to their homes, and to keep the peace. Or, if it did occur to them, no one had sufficient courage to take this reasonable course; but, swift to shed blood, the Riot Act is hastily read, (so it is affirmed,)—not one, perhaps, of all the crowd being aware of the proceeding, or understanding what it meant,—and the volunteers, a feeble company of some eighteen or twenty men, are ordered at once to fire upon the people. More sensible and less sanguinary men would have tried the effect of blank cartridges before proceeding to the fatal extremity of the rifle ball; but no such prudent and temperate proceeding was thought of, and the volunteers, under the direction of the magistrates, sent a deadly volley into the midst of the advancing crowd. This was repeated; and between thirty and forty, killed or grievously wounded, fell to the ground. It wanted only this to bring on a fearful crisis, which might have been avoided.

The black people of our colonies are by no means

sanguinary or revengeful. Long years of injustice and oppression have shown them to be enduring, patient, and forgiving. Before emancipation, and since, I have had opportunities for observation; and it is a fact which their general history in every British colony bears out, that neither towards each other, nor towards their oppressors, do they manifest anything like a vindictive spirit. But they are, like all other men, capable of being aroused and excited by accumulated provocation to deeds of fury and blood: and at Morant Bay the provocation was supplied. Rendered nearly desperate already by multiplied wrongs, they could not tamely stand by, and see friends and relations wantonly shot down at their feet by dozens; and, infuriated beyond all control by the savage and murderous attack made upon them, they rushed upon the aggressors, and inflicted a merciless and terrible retaliation that will not soon be forgotten. Several of the volunteers who fired upon them first fell victims to their fury; and then the Magistrates and others, who had sheltered within the court-house, and from thence continued firing upon the crowd, after the building had been either accidentally or designedly set on fire, were driven from their refuge, and killed in detail, as they fell into the hands of their pursuers.

Frightful stories were circulated concerning indignities and barbarities which the Negroes were said to have practised upon the dead bodies of their victims. These stories were gathered up and repeated by Mr. Eyre, and had currency given to them in his despatches. His conduct in this matter is altogether indefensible; for, being on the spot, he must have known that these were mere fabrications, and that no such savage mutilations of the slaughtered whites took place. This was amply proved before the Commissioners; and, further than this, it was proved beyond all doubt, to the lasting disgrace of .the British army, that the revolting barbarities really inflicted upon the dead were practised by British soldiers, and officers bearing her Majesty's commission in the army and navy. I was assured by a highly respectable gentleman that, with the exception of cutting off a finger of the Baron von Ketelholdt, to obtain possession of a valuable ring which he wore at the time of his death, there was no mutilation of any of the bodies beyond that occasioned by the blows which caused their death. My informant witnessed the outbreak, being in the Morant Bay court-house with the unfortunate Baron and his companions; and he also saw the bodies of the slain, and inspected them afterwards. One circumstance occurred, which perhaps served to give some colour of truth to the story concerning indignities offered to the remains of the slaughtered victims. This, however, was not attributable to the rioters, but to the neglect of the friends of the unfortunate dead, who were too thoroughly panic-stricken to be capable of taking any kind of action, even after all traces of the rioters had long disappeared from the town; in consequence of which the bodies of the victims were left unburied and exposed, until one of them, that of Mr. Herschell, attracted the notice of the vulture crows, which are always flying about in search of prey. These ravenous birds attacked the senseless remains, plucking out the eyes, and otherwise disfiguring the body. This was the only case of mutilation that occurred.

Mr. Eyre, in one of his despatches to Mr. Cardwell, anxious to heap obloquy upon the black portion of the population, makes the following statement, after he had spent some time at Morant Bay, and had abundant opportunity of learning the truth :—

"The most frightful atrocities were perpetrated. The island curate of Bath, the Rev. Mr. Herschell, is said to have had his tongue cut out whilst still alive, and an attempt is said to have been made to skin him. One person (Mr. Charles Price, a black gentleman, formerly a member of Assembly) was ripped open, and his entrails taken out. One gentleman (Lieut. Hall, of the Volunteers) is said to have been pushed into an outbuilding, which was then set on fire, and kept there till he was ultimately roasted alive. Many were said to have had their eyes scooped out; heads were cleft open, and the brains taken out. The Baron's fingers were cut off, and carried away as trophies by the murderers. Some bodies were half burnt, others horribly battered. Indeed, the whole outrage could only be paralleled by the atrocities of the Indian mutiny. The women, as usual on such occasions, were even more brutal and barbarous than the men; the only redeeming trait being that, so far as we could learn, no ladies or children had as yet been injured."

Mr. Eyre had been at Morant Bay several times before he wrote this, and could have learned the truth without difficulty; and it is significant that, possessing full opportunity of testing the facts, he is careful to say concerning most of these frightful stories, "*It is said*" that so and so took place. Unfortunately for Mr. Eyre's regard for truth, it was proved before the Royal Commission that this statement was incorrect in nearly every particular. Mr. Herschell's tongue was *not* cut out, nor was any attempt made to skin him. Mr. Price was not ripped open, nor his entrails taken out. Lieut. Hall was not roasted alive, but killed by a shot in the throat, during the riot, when the volunteers were firing on the Negroes from the court-house, and the people were firing in return. One only of the Baron's fingers was cut off, to obtain the ring that adorned it. No eyes were scooped out, no brains taken out; and there is no evidence that the women were more barbarous than the men. But there is evidence that the life of the Rector was saved by a woman; that one of his wounded sons, who afterwards died, was carefully attended by another woman, at some risk to herself; and that several others were protected and assisted by black women.

The rioters, having taken vengeance upon their assailants, separated immediately, and left the town, doing no further violence to either person or property; the riot having lasted not more than four or five hours. But in several other localities in the parish bodies of disorderly people assembled, stimulated, no doubt, by exaggerated accounts of what had taken place at Morant Bay; and several stores and houses were plundered. In two or three cases, also, ill-disposed persons took advantage of the occasion to retaliate upon those who had rendered themselves unpopular in various ways,—one white man named Hire being killed, and others severely beaten.

Not one word can be said in apology for these lawless deeds; and the savage violence which marked the conduct of the mob at Morant Bay, and in one or two other places, though not without provocation, must be strongly reprobated, even by those who take the most favourable view of their case. But it is right and proper that the truth, the whole truth, as far as it can be ascertained, should appear; and that blame in just proportion should rest where it is due. Many of the newspapers of the day gave currency to the most exaggerated statements concerning the events that took place; and not only were the Negroes concerned in them held up before the world as some of the most revolting monsters of cruelty that ever existed, but slanders of the vilest kind were heaped upon the black and coloured races generally; and multitudes, who have not been better informed, yet cherish views and feelings concerning them, in consequence of such misrepresentations, which are not to be reconciled either with charity or truth.

The facts concerning this riot, falsely magnified into a rebellion, are few and simple. A number of persons, smarting under grievous wrongs, assembled together in a tumultuous manner; but there is no proof that they offered violence to any one. It is said they threw stones; but it is a remarkable fact that not one person has been brought forward that was hurt or hit by these missiles; and it is probably a fabrication got up to justify or excuse the sanguinary deed which brought on the fatal collision. Too much prominence cannot be given to the fact that the Custos, and those associated with him, performed the first act of violence by firing upon the crowd. Up to this point no person had been injured, no violence offered to any individual. If the people were transgressing the limits of right, and transgressing the law, in assembling as they had done, the Custos, or the Rector, or some of the parties in the court-house, men of superior standing and intelligence. should have gone out and remonstrated with the unlettered and misguided assemblage; and, pointing out wherein they were wrong, should have given them suitable advice. This was no more than might reasonably have been expected from magistrates and clergymen, two of the latter being present. But without a word of counsel, or any attempt to turn an excited people from any wrongful purposes they might have in view, they were at once fired upon, and many of them killed and wounded.

This act of the authorities is totally indefensible on any ground, and it is the pivot upon which the whole case turns. But for this there would have been no riot,

no bloodshed, no burning of the court-house, no martial
law, and none of those terrible atrocities which followed,
and excited the indignation of the whole Christian
world. The authorities were the first aggressors, and
upon them justly rests the responsibility of the outbreak. They first shed blood, wantonly and unnecessarily; and the people upon whom they ordered the
volunteers to fire would have been more or less than
men, had they not retaliated in the way they did.
However much we may deplore and condemn the
slaughter of Baron Ketelholdt and his associates, they
certainly brought destruction upon themselves, and
became the victims of their own foolish and guilty disregard of the sanctity of human life. The act of
firing successive volleys upon a mob who had done so
little to provoke—nothing to deserve—it, can scarcely
be classed in any other category than that of murder,
and would probably have been pronounced to be such
by an unbiassed British jury.

One gentleman, Dr. Major, who was in the court-
house when the attack was made upon it, fell into the
hands of the rioters; but no injury was done to him,
as he was one who had always manifested a kindly
sympathy with the labouring class in their wrongs and
oppressions. They singled out for retaliation those whom
they regarded as their oppressors, or the tools of oppression, and offered no violence or injury to others. The
number of victims who perished in the outbreak was
eighteen killed, thirty-one wounded,—including two or
three who for different reasons were maltreated in
different localities by mobs who took the opportunity
afforded by the prevailing confusion to visit upon
wrong-doers the injuries formerly received at their
hands. The volunteers fell in a conflict in which they
commenced the shedding of blood; and well-nigh all

the others who were killed had rendered themselves obnoxious to the people's vengeance by the wrongs they had contributed to heap upon them. That so few were injured, when the mob were masters of the situation and had the town and its inhabitants completely at their mercy for many hours, shows that they could be moderate even when most infuriated, and completely falsifies the representations in which a part of the press delighted to indulge as to the ferocity and barbarity of the blacks, and their intention to massacre the white and coloured people. They could easily have burnt the town and destroyed many lives, if they had been so disposed; but having, in a sudden paroxysm of fury, smitten down those by whom they had been assailed in a cowardly and sanguinary manner, they retired, satisfied with the transient victory they had achieved, and the vengeance they had inflicted. It was like a whirlwind, brief in its duration, but terrible in its results; affording another illustration of the truth which West India planters have been so slow and unwilling to recognise, that the Negro is human, swayed by the same emotions and passions as his brethren with a paler skin, and requiring at their hands treatment suitable to the high and immortal nature with which his Creator has endowed him.

A lamentable want of decision and promptitude seems to have marked the conduct of the Jamaica authorities in relation to the outbreak. Governor Eyre received Baron Ketelholdt's despatch, reporting the riotous disposition of the Negroes, and asking for military aid, at eight o'clock on the 11th of October. Within an hour or two after that, the letter or petition of Paul Bogle and others was placed in his hands. He must have been blind indeed not to see that a dangerous collision between the Magistrates and the people was imminent. Had he at once sent off a dozen or twenty men by land, they could have reached Morant Bay in four hours, and their presence would have been sufficient to check the rioters; or if he had at once caused a small military force to embark in a steamer from Port Royal, they could have been landed in time to prevent the disturbance. But, contenting himself with merely requesting the Commander of the forces to send on a hundred men to Morant Bay, without troubling himself further about the matter, he betook himself to his dinner party in the mountains. Such was the culpable indifference that prevailed, that no movement was made until the following day. Then, some twenty-four hours after the receipt of the despatch, the "Wolverine" ship of war was leisurely got under weigh; and, arriving at Morant Bay with a military force, discovered that the mischief had occurred, which a more prompt attention to duty on the part of the civil and military authorities might have prevented. It does not appear that any official notice was ever taken of this culpable apathy, so as to lay the blame where it was justly due for such unaccountable and, as it proved, fatal delay.

CHAPTER IV.

But if there was a want of promptitude in taking measures to prevent the outbreak, there was certainly no lack of energy in making reprisals. Fearful indeed has been the penalty exacted from a whole community for the misdeeds of a few persons. A thousand dwellings given to the flames, and a thousand homes wantonly desolated; a multitude of widows and fatherless children left without a shelter, and recklessly plundered; and a long catalogue of frightful murders and inhuman cruelties, rivalling in their details the fiendish ingenuity with which North American savages torture their victims,—bear witness to the ferocious barbarity with which Governor Eyre, and the military and naval officers acting under his direction, retaliated upon an unarmed and unresisting people the deeds of violence in which only a few of them had taken any part. On receiving intelligence of the riot at Morant Bay, and the death of Custos Von Ketelholdt and his fellow-sufferers, Mr. Eyre immediately summoned a council of war, at which it was determined to place the county of Surrey under martial law, excepting only the city of Kingston. Military detachments and vessels of war were sent on to the scene of the disturbance; bodies of volunteers were enrolled; and a chief hangman, called the Provost-Marshal, was commissioned, in the person of Mr. Gordon Duberry Ramsay, of infamous notoriety. Governor Eyre himself hastened to the spot, taking care, however, in the exercise of that discretion which is said to be the better part of valour, not to travel by land, as a man like the Earl of

E

Mulgrave or Sir John Keene would have done; but keeping his person secure within the bulwarks of a war steamer, where no stray bullet was at all likely to reach him, and prepared, as results abundantly showed, to " cry havoc, and let slip the dogs of war ! " Seldom have · these significant words received a more fearful comment. Havoc attended upon his footsteps; and, like the hungry hounds of Cuba, the savage hordes which he let loose upon the people without any check to their ferocity, and with no instructions but to ravage and destroy, gorged themselves with blood.

The official despatches sent to the Colonial Office by Governor Eyre himself, containing the reports furnished by military and naval officers, and commanders of the volunteer detachments, related such deeds of cruelty, breathed such remorseless vengeance, and boasted of such wholesale and indiscriminate slaughter, as to call forth, as soon as they appeared, one general burst of indignation from the religious public and the newspaper press of Great Britain, and elicited loud cries of shame and reprobation from the newspapers of other countries. Some of these boastful statements were afterwards disclaimed, or retracted, by their authors, and others modified and toned down, so far · as they could contrive to do it without making the direct acknowledgment that they had attempted to obtain a cheap kind of glory by putting forth wilful falsities, and boasting of imaginary victories over defenceless men, and women, and children. But enough remains, fully substantiated on oath before the Royal Commission, to make it manifest that the alleged *atrocities* of the riotous Negroes had been far outdone by British officers and British soldiers and sailors; and that the designation *" monsters of cruelty "* was far more applicable to the whites than to the blacks. Many of the barbarities practised by the white troops, the volunteers, the blacks of the West India regiments, and the Maroons, never came fully to light; and many doubtless are altogether hidden with the murdered in the hasty graves to which they were ruthlessly consigned, until that day when all secrets will be revealed; but quite sufficient was established during the investigations of the Royal Commissioners, and not unfrequently by the reluctant testimony drawn from the perpetrators themselves, to show that during that reign of terror called " martial law," extending over thirty days, the east end of Jamaica became a pandemonium of crime; and deeds were enacted under British authority, and in the name of Britain's Sovereign, that equal, if they do not exceed, the worst excesses of the Russians in Poland, and fix a stain upon the honour of the nation that ages will not wipe away.

Two days after the outbreak, Governor Eyre proceeded to Morant Bay, and at once commissioned and sent out his agents of destruction, eager for the slaughter. It is a very significant fact, and illustrates the character and disposition of the man, that the first life taken under the newly proclaimed martial law was taken in the presence of the Governor himself, under his own directions, and almost under his own hand. The Council of War was held on the morning of the 13th of October, at which it was determined to proclaim martial law. This was done; and the same afternoon Mr. Eyre embarked for Morant Bay, from whence he went on at night, in the " Onyx " gun-boat, under the command of the notorious Lieutenant Brand, to Port Morant, a distance of some six miles; and by morning light on the 14th were initiated those scenes of slaughter, which marked the history of the several succeeding weeks.

At Port Morant, a terror-stricken person, named

Hague, one of the Custom House officials, complained to the Governor, and those who were with him, concerning a black man in the village, named Fleming, that he had held out some threats against himself. This was enough for men who were athirst for blood. It was midnight when the Governor and his party landed at Port Morant, and immediately Captain Ross and twenty-five men were sent to capture Fleming. It was sufficient proof that he was no leader of rebels, that he was found quietly at home in his own house, and not associated with any armed force; nor was there the slightest reason to believe that he was in any way mixed up with the tragic events which had transpired at Morant Bay. But there, on the spot, in the dark hours of the morning, a pretended court-martial was improvised. It consisted of a Mr. Lewis, just made an officer of volunteers; a Mr. Fyfe, a stipendiary magistrate, newly appointed to command the Maroons; and Captain Hunt, the Governor's own secretary. A few minutes sufficed for this mockery of a British tribunal to pronounce the man guilty; for the Governor was close at hand, looking on, with that pattern soldier, Brigadier Nelson, waiting anxiously for the man's conviction; and before the poor fellow was well awake he was sentenced to be executed forthwith. Dragged from his bed in the middle of the night, and placed at once on trial, before men bent upon putting him to death, there was neither time nor opportunity for defence. Immediately the man was condemned, Mr. Eyre, the representative of England's Queen, took upon him the office of provost-marshal, bearing an active part in this cruel outrage. He wrote a note to Mr. Brand, and sent it to him on board the gun-boat "Onyx," directing that worthy to come ashore immediately, and bring a rope with him, and perform the functions of assistant hangman. How dignified and fitting this in a British Governor, and the commander of one of Her Majesty's vessels of war! Such an office and such employment were perfectly congenial to Lieutenant Brand; and he at once obeyed the summons, and hastened ashore to perform the dishonourable task assigned to him. Such a scene was surely never exhibited in a British colony before, amongst all the strange doings our colonies have witnessed : a naval commander, whose rank is supposed to be that of a gentleman, invading the unenviable province of Calcraft's assistant; and His Excellency, the representative of Britain's Sovereign, invading that of Calcraft himself, superintending and directing the details of this heartless execution. It is well that the sun had not yet risen, to shed his rays upon such a deed of shame, and that the whole of this repulsive procedure was shrouded in the darkness that best befitted it.

No time was lost in erecting a gallows, but one was improvised for the occasion. The thirst for life could not wait for customary forms; so the bough of a neighbouring tree was selected for the purpose. The poor victim, scarcely conscious of the doom awaiting him, was tied, and hurried to the spot by the lieutenant hangman and his helpers, the rope placed upon his throat, and the other end thrown over and made fast to the branch of the tree. A door, hastily torn from its hinges, was made to serve the purpose of a scaffold; and this being kicked from under him, the wretched man was swung off to die. But, done in such haste, the cruel deed is not well done; it is sadly and cruelly bungled. We will, to avoid mistake, give the remainder of the tragedy in the words of Mr. Lewis, one of the members of the court-martial that condemned Fleming, as given by him upon oath, very reluctantly, before the Royal Commissioners :—

"He was hung upon a tree, and the trap was a door, a temporary one. This being taken away, the bough gave way, and his feet slightly touched the ground. Lieutenant Brand went up to him with a revolver, and fired twice into him; and a soldier then came up, and fired into his breast, and that was the end of Fleming."

And with that red hand, stained with this cruel deed, this man Brand went, soon after, to preside at the mock trial of George William Gordon! Who can be surprised that the result should be what it was? Brand boasted of this transaction, as if he had performed some feat honourable to an officer in Her Majesty's navy: "He had the pleasure of hanging the first damned rebel, named Fleming, at Port Morant; but nothing would give him greater pleasure than to hang this damned son of a ——, Gordon." Only that it is a fact proved beyond all doubt, it could scarcely be believed that, in any part of the dominions of Queen Victoria, a man of such low, brutal nature and language could be allowed to sit as president of a court that disposed of the lives of several hundreds of British subjects. In the hands of such a person, poor Gordon had no more chance of escape, or of being justly dealt with, than if he had been in the jaws of a tiger.

All the time this bad deed was being enacted, Governor Eyre was looking on; feasting his eyes upon the cruel slaughter of a man who had been fifteen years in the employment of the gentleman whose servant he was, when dragged from his bed to be put to death. Having thus with his own hand participated in initiating an unparalleled series of crimes and murders,—for his hand penned the note which brought the assistant hangman with his rope to perfect the tragedy,—he returned to Morant Bay, where similar scenes occurred in the course of the day, to be succeeded by hundreds more, until they were finally checked by the indignant voice of an outraged people.

"There can be no doubt," says Mr. Gorrie, "that the trial and execution of Fleming, under the eye of Mr. Eyre himself, had a most important effect upon the mode in which affairs were afterwards conducted. Many of the chief actors in the subsequent proceedings were present: General Nelson, who was the officer in command; Lieutenant Brand, who presided at the court-martial at Morant Bay; Colonel Lewis, (militia,) who presided, or sat, on courts-martial there or elsewhere; Captain Hunt, who presided at courts-martial at Port Antonio; and Mr. Fyfe, who became chief of the Maroons; and all learned that their proceedings gave satisfaction to the Governor.

"At the worst, the unhappy wretch Fleming had only been guilty of brawling or rioting, without injuring any individual, assuming the charges against him to have been proved. He was not accused of having been at Morant Bay when the justices and volunteers were killed: he was not taken in arms, or at the head of any organized body of men, offering resistance to constituted authority. The offence of which he was accused had been committed, if at all, before the proclamation of martial law, the date of which was the 13th of October, so that his trial by court-martial was illegal: that is to say, the Governor of the island, Mr. Eyre, the three military men who constituted the court-martial, General Nelson, who ordered and approved of the proceedings, and Lieutenant Brand, who was induced by Mr. Eyre to act as executioner, took upon themselves duties which could only be performed by the civil law Judges and ordinary instruments of the law, and put a subject of Her Majesty to death, whom they had no authority to try. Moreover, the mode in which the proceedings were carried out, was singularly repulsive, and calculated, when approved of by the Governor, to make military men regardless of human life and the requirements of justice. Fleming was apprehended about four o'clock in the morning: he got no opportunity of preparing his defence; he was at once tried, and executed the same morning by six o'clock. Even if he had been the worst rebel that ever shook a throne, this haste would have been indecent and repulsive. But thus to seize and hurry to death an obscure subject of Her Majesty, who was not caught in any overt act of resistance to authority, is worthy of the utmost condemnation."

Thus it was that Governor Eyre himself inaugurated a series of butcheries, since pronounced by the highest legal authority of the realm to be as much at variance with the law as they are shocking to humanity. The military force brought to Morant Bay was at once marched off in different detachments, overspreading the country; but nowhere did they find any indications of the widespread rebellion which was made the pretext for the atrocities committed by the military themselves. In no direction did they find any armed force of rebels. They encountered no resistance : they found no collection of ammunition or arms of any kind. Moving in larger bodies, or in smaller companies of two or three, or half-a-dozen, not a single shot was fired at them, no hand was anywhere raised to oppose them. The pretence of a rebellion and a rebellious conspiracy against the Government, was as impudent a fabrication as was ever attempted to be imposed upon a credulous community. After the outbreak at Morant Bay, provoked, as we have seen, by the indiscretion of the authorities, a riotous mob assembled in two or three different directions; but everywhere the appearance of the military was sufficient to disperse them; and the gallantry of these military heroes was expended in making war upon a defenceless and unresisting people, including the sick, and lame, and blind, and women and children, and burning down the dwelling-houses of thousands who were as ignorant of all that had taken place at Morant

Bay as if they had been the inhabitants of another country. Two days after the proclamation of martial law, Governor Eyre himself pronounced the rebellion to be at an end; and, in his despatch to the Colonial Secretary, dated October 20th, only one week after martial law was in force, he wrote: "No stand has ever been made against the troops; and though we are not only in complete military occupation, but have traversed with troops all the disturbed districts, not a single casualty has befallen any of our soldiers or sailors, and they are all in good health." Several days later, the Governor, in another despatch, writes: "Even in the district to the eastward, where the rebellion actually broke out, there was no attempt to resist; an organized force, of only thirty-five men, marched through the heart of the disturbed district, from Port Morant to the Rhine, beyond Bath." Thus Governor Eyre himself shows, what was amply proved before the Commissioners, that there was no rebellion—nothing beyond a sudden local riot—to sanction in any degree the havoc and bloodshed to which the country and its defenceless inhabitants were given up for several weeks by the man whose office bound him to be their protector.

From British soldiers and sailors, especially from British military and naval officers, who are supposed to be, from their education and profession, gentlemen and men of honour, we were entitled to expect something like the exercise of moderation and humanity, when dealing with an unarmed and unresisting people. But whether it was that the Governor had animated them with the same ferocious spirit he had himself displayed in disposing of the unhappy man Fleming, or that other influences were brought to bear upon them, certain it is, that officers and men alike seemed, when let loose upon the defenceless black people, thousands of whom were innocent of all intention to do wrong, to be more like incarnate fiends than men ; revelling in cruelty and slaughter, and carrying destruction and ruin wherever they came.   The gallantry of the troops and volunteers was loudly boasted of, but with wonderfully small reason.   This boasted gallantry was certainly not displayed in meeting any attack of a brave and determined foe, on somewhat like equal terms, but in shooting down unarmed and unresisting men and boys, who, frightened at the sight of a red coat, were flying to the shelter of the bush, not caring to trust themselves to the tender mercies of these heroes ; and in turning out feeble women and their little children from their homes, and desolating those homes with fire.   In no instance was a hand uplifted to oppose them ; yet these wonderfully heroic soldiers left a thousand families without the shelter of a roof.   If ever a body of men earned a title to be branded as cowards, surely none can dispute the title in the case of the heartless body of destroyers let loose upon the parish of St. Thomas-in-the-East by Mr. Eyre.   A gentleman who accompanied the first detachment of troops that marched through what was called " the disturbed district," on the next day after the proclamation of martial law, under the command of Ensign Cullen, who was afterwards tried on a charge of murder, told me that, although they met with not the slightest resistance, such was the ferocity of these men, that if he had not been present to exercise some restraint upon them, they would not have left a single black person alive, or a Negro dwelling undestroyed, on all the line of their march between Port Morant and Bath.   As it was, blood and fire marked their course.   The accounts given by some of the officers of their own exploits, and published in the newspapers or in the Governor's despatches, caused men to stand aghast at the excesses they described; and it was these, and these alone, that called forth such an outburst of indignation from the British public as rendered it necessary for the Government at home at once to supersede Governor Eyre, and appoint a Royal Commission to investigate the doings of the authorities in Jamaica.

Colonel Hobbs was one who particularly distinguished himself by what, with sad perversion of language, was called " his gallantry," in making war upon a noncombatant people, and by the manner in which he boasted of his deeds,—deeds which would fix upon any man a lasting stigma of infamy. Amongst the earliest despatches made public, there was one from this officer, commanding a British regiment, in which occurs the following passage, scarcely to be paralleled for its cool and ineffable atrocity :—" About daylight this morning, in passing through the village of Cross Roads, where the rebels destroyed every thing, I found a number of special constables, who had captured a number of prisoners from the rebel camp." (A mere figure of speech this, as no traces of the existence of any rebel camp were ever discovered.) " Finding their guilt clear," (without any trial or defence,) "and unable to take or leave them, I had them all shot. The constables then hung them upon trees, eleven in number. Their countenances were all diabolical, and they never flinched the very slightest." Thus, without even a form of trial, simply as a matter of convenience,—for he could not take them or leave them,—this British officer puts eleven British subjects to death, who were probably as innocent of all rebellion as himself; and, not content with simply murdering them, he causes the dead bodies to be treated with insulting and revolting indignity. One of the offences alleged against the black rioters at Morant

Bay was, that they treated their dead victims with barbarous outrage, by wantonly mutilating and heaping
indignity upon the bodies of the slain.   This was clearly
disproved; but here we have a white gentleman, and
an officer high in command in Her Majesty's service,
boasting of doing foul dishonour to the dead bodies of
his slaughtered victims.   After destroying life by shooting them, in a spirit of barbarism which would have
been disgraceful in a North American savage, he caused
the senseless remains to be hung up on the sur-
rounding trees.   This occurred at a place called Chiego
Market.

Next day this gentleman, Colonel Hobbs, shot nine
more at Fonthill, and after that sixteen at Coley; and
so little care was taken to ascertain anything concerning the guilt or innocence of these slaughtered victims,
that the officers acting under Hobbs admitted to the
Commissioners, when examined upon oath, that of
twenty-eight they put to death, they did not even know
the names of eighteen.   As none of them were taken
in arms, or actual resistance to constituted authority,
we can understand how very little trouble was taken to
discover that these poor creatures had done anything
deserving death, when even their names remained
unknown.

Colonel Hobbs not only dishonoured the dead, but,
with sacrilegious impiety, he did what he could to
dishonour the places devoted to prayer and the worship
of God; causing the dead bodies of some he had killed
to be hung up to the rafters, and left there to decay,
until the friends of the murdered came by stealth to
take them away and consign them to their more
appropriate resting-place in the dust.   As if lost to
all shame and decency, he boasted in his despatches of
the methods he adopted to add refinement to cruelty

and murder. He said, "I shot nine of the Fonthill rebels in a chapel, where their leader commenced with prayers, and ended with blasphemy and sedition; and I there adopted a plan which struck immense terror into these wicked men, far more than death; which is, I caused them to hang each other. They entreated to be shot, to avoid this, which appears to me to be far more dreadful an ordeal to them than death."

"This description," says Mr. Gorrie, "scarcely does justice to the mode of punishment adopted. Before the victims were hung, they were first shot; and the general body of prisoners, whether tried or not, were ordered to take up the bleeding bodies of their former friends and neighbours, and hang them to the rafters of the building where together they had engaged in the worship of God."

This Colonel Hobbs shot thirteen men at Monklands, all at once, thinking no doubt it was capital sport to make a *battue* of his fellow-men. He had a trench dug, and made the unfortunate men kneel with their backs towards it. The soldiers drawn up for the purpose fired at the sound of the bugle, or the word of command. Some, not killed, cried out with pain; and the soldiers ordered them with brutal curses to shut their mouths, or they would blow their brains out. They gave two or three who were wounded a close shot to finish them. Even after this one George Rankin remained alive. The soldiers were in the act of throwing the earth into the trench to fill it up, covering both the living and the dead, when Hobbs gave orders that the pickaxe should be used to finish Rankin. "It is capable of proof," says Mr. Gorrie, "by living witnesses, that the brutal order was executed, and the man killed with the pickaxe; but if not, he was buried alive."

When writing his despatches, in which he made a

boast of his sanguinary deeds, Colonel Hobbs little thought that ere long he would be compelled to appear before the Royal Commissioners, and testify to these things upon oath. Such, however, was the case, and there he was made to swear to his own infamy. A short time after, either shame or remorse, or both together, overwhelmed him, and his reason became unsettled; and embarking, after the lapse of a few weeks, for England, this butcher of the innocent jumped overboard, and found a watery grave. Apologists for the wrong doings of those days have said, "Hobbs was mad when he wrote his despatches, and perpetrated the cruelties those documents described." Should a madman, such as it is said that Hobbs was, have been let loose upon the poor defenceless Negroes to ravage and destroy? That he became mad is very probable: this was doubtless the result of the shame and remorse which overwhelmed him, when the outcry of an indignant public aroused him to a sense of the enormities of which he had been guilty; and was permitted in the operations of that retributive Providence which often causes the sins of the wicked to come upon their own heads, and cuts off the bloody and deceitful man before he has lived out half his days.

When before the Royal Commissioners, he manifestly laboured under a painful sense of the infamy which his boasted deeds had brought upon him; and he endeavoured to shelter himself under a letter penned by a man of kindred spirit, an officer named Elkington, who was acting as Deputy Adjutant-General. Revelling in the scent of blood, this man wrote to Colonel Hobbs, October 18th, a letter which he (Hobbs) regarded as official, urging him on to the slaughter of the Negroes. It was couched in the following terms:—

"DEAR COLONEL,

"I SEND you an order to push on at once to Stony Gut: but I trust you are there already. Hole is doing splendid service with his men all about Manchioneal, and shooting every black man who cannot account for himself. (Sixty on line of march.) Nelson is at Port Antonio, hanging like fun by court-martial. I hope you will not send in any prisoners. Civil law can do nothing. Lots of food for you at Gardens. Send for boots if you need them at Newcastle, and write to me if you want ammunition as well at Newcastle, for I will send more to them. Do punish the blackguards well.

"Yours in haste,

"J. ELKINGTON, D.A.G."

Who would have thought it possible that such ruffianism could be found amongst gentlemen of the British army? Who could have imagined that there were to be found men holding commissions in Her Majesty's service brutal enough to write such a letter, or base enough to act upon such sanguinary instructions?

Colonel Hobbs belonged to the 6th Regiment of Foot, the officers and men of which distinguished themselves in the bloody doings of those days, in Jamaica, beyond their fellows. It would be scarcely justice to this *gallant* body of British soldiers that their heroic deeds should not be made known, or that the *glorious victories* achieved by them over defenceless women and boys, and the blind, and lame, and infirm, should not be recorded. The following facts were testified on oath before the Royal Commissioners.

At Fonthill, on Friday, October the 20th, some soldiers belonging to this *gallant* 6th Regiment, slept in the cottage of a Negro named Cherrington, who treated them with kind hospitality, furnishing them with dry clothes and a dinner. On Sunday, two days after, two of them returned to the cottage; and while the wife was absent for a few moments in a neighbour's house, without the slightest provocation, they brutally murdered the husband Cherrington, and then proceeded to plunder the house. After driving out the children whom they had made fatherless, they were about to set fire to the cottage, when the opportune arrival upon the spot of a neighbouring constable prevented this consummation of their villany. The widow produced to the Commissioners the bullet with which her husband was killed.

At Stony Gut a boy was wantonly shot by Lieutenant Oxley's party, when they visited that locality. The little fellow had unexpectedly come upon the military; and when he saw them, he turned round and attempted to run and escape, when these *gallant* soldiers fired upon and killed the lad. He had not been away from home, and had taken no part in the riot at Morant Bay. The body lay unburied until the vultures gathered about it, when the neighbours summoned courage to hide away the festering remains in the earth.

At a very pleasant and flourishing village, called Somerset, there resided an old man named Richard Graham, blind and infirm through old age, so that he could not move about without being led. On Tuesday, the 17th of October, when the soldiers of the *gallant* 6th were displaying their courage in burning the houses of the helpless inhabitants, this blind old man was found sitting quietly at the door of his cottage, in the sunshine, supposing that his age and infirmities would be a sufficient protection from violence. But the *gallant* 6th respected neither age nor infirmity. It was enough for them that any person had a black skin; that was sufficient proof in their eyes that he must be a rebel.   A nephew of the old man who lived with him, when he saw these heroes approaching, hid himself in the bush until the soldiers should take their departure.   From his hiding-place close at hand, the young man heard a gun fired in the yard; and on coming forth after the destroyers were gone, he proceeded to the spot, and found the old man dead.   These brave soldiers of Her Majesty's 6th Regiment had gained a distinguished victory over the blind old man, and shot him; and to celebrate and complete their triumph, they had set fire to the poor man's house, and the body was partly consumed in the flames.   The nephew and a son of the old man buried his charred remains.   Both their houses were also burnt, after being plundered by the soldiers, who carried off all their clothes, even those belonging to their little children.

About the same time, a party of these white soldiers went to Garbrand Hall, and entered the house of a black man, named James Johnson, who had just returned from Morant Bay, whither he had been taken as a prisoner, but had been released on the interposition of a Mr. Miller, who had previously known him, and the good character he bore.   When the soldiers came to the house, his wife, Catherine Johnson, was sitting at the door, with her baby in her arms; the husband, who had just come in from his ground, having gone to an adjacent building to obtain a light for his pipe.   The soldiers inquired of the woman where her husband was, and she replied, "He is gone to the kitchen."   While she was speaking, he made his appearance; when the soldiers, turning to him, inquired if he was one of the rebels?   He said, "No;" and, as the word fell from his lips, they fired, and shot him dead;—only the wife and their little son were present.   The ruffians then set

F

the house on fire, and the body of the murdered man
was likely to have been burned inside, before the newly
widowed woman could summon help.   Two young men,
a cousin and brother-in-law, came and rescued the body
from the flames, and dug a grave, and buried it.   The
bereaved woman, thus wantonly deprived of her home
and her husband, found shelter with another widow,
whose husband had been slaughtered at Morant Bay.

At Monklands, two men were shot by these brave
soldiers, one of whom was William Shann.   He was a
lame man, helpless from numerous sores, so that it was
with difficulty he could move about.   As these heroes
of the 6th Regiment went past, he was lying on a bench
at the front of his cottage.   His mother thus described
the scene, in her evidence given before the Commissioners :—"Two soldiers came to the door-mouth : I
rose up, and said, 'Sirs, it is a sick person ; it is my son
that is sick.'   Just as I said so, the other one fire off,
and the young man drop down.   They said afterwards
they were truly sorry it was an innocent person, but
they can't help it, it was done already, they only do their
duty.   They say they thought it was a rebel ; they were
very sorry, but they can't help it."

On the same day, at Mount Libanus, two soldiers of
the same battalion seized a woman, Mrs. Rebecca Telfer,
and demanded from her her marriage ring.   She said it
was lost ; but one of the soldiers said he did not believe
her statement, and cried out, " Shoot her ! shoot her ! "
She bent down, and said, " Good massa, don't shoot me,
for I don't know any thing at all.   If you shoot me, who
is to take care of my little children ? "   She begged
hard for her life, and gave them two shillings, which was
all the money she had, to induce them to let her go.
Her house had already been burnt down, and she was
sheltering in a small kitchen that had escaped the flames.

The soldiers then seized upon her, and endeavoured to force her to enter the small building with them. She resisted them with all her might; when, just at that juncture, her father-in-law, John Telfer, who lived near at hand, appeared upon the scene, having heard the noise she made in struggling with them. The soldiers, irritated at his appearance to interfere with their vile purposes, instantly seized their rifles, and shot him down; and she took the opportunity of their releasing her, to snatch up her two children, and escape into the bush.

On the 22nd of October, four white soldiers were taken by a Mr. Christopher Codrington to his house at Rose Garden, where they took dinner. When they returned, in the evening, to David Mayne's shop at Long Bay, two constables were there with two prisoners, named James Sparkes and Johnson Speed. They proceeded at once to tie Sparkes to a tree, and gave him a hundred lashes. They then tied up Johnson Speed, and had given him eighty-five lashes, when the cat broke. One of the soldiers ran into the shop, and brought a horse-whip to finish the flogging; but the other interfered, and prevented him, saying it was not the right thing to beat a man with. One of the bystanders was here asked by the soldiers whether the man Speed had done any thing during the disturbances; evidently seeking a pretext for further villany. He replied that, when Mr. Hinchelwood's house was burning, Speed was there. The soldier who was flogging him then said, "Where is my rifle?" The man cried out, "Lord, I don't do nothing, and I going to dead." The soldier levelled his rifle, and fired; but either it contained no ball, or he had missed. He loaded again, and fired, hitting the poor victim in the middle of his back, as he was tied to the tree. Another soldier then stepped up, as he

dropped writhing upon the ground, as far as the cords
would allow him to fall, and, putting his rifle to the man's
ear, scattered his brains all around.   These were soldiers
belonging to the second battalion of Her Majesty's 6th
Regiment of Foot,—" *the gallant 6th.*"

The 6th Regiment was greatly lauded in some of the
island newspapers, and the gallantry of its officers and
men made the subject of high-sounding praise; as if
they had bravely met and overcome some hostile force,
vastly superior to themselves.   Whereas, they never
heard a shot fired except by themselves, and never saw
an enemy, unless we may regard as enemies a few terrified black men and women and children; who, totally
unarmed, and never dreaming of resistance, fled in terror
at the sight of their red coats.   All the laurels they ever
won in Jamaica were gained by shooting down a flying
people, and making war upon the old, and blind, and
lame, turning helpless families out of their homes, and
burning down their dwellings.   Wherever this regiment
goes, its gallant deeds ought to be proclaimed, that due
honour may be rendered to the heroic conquerors of
feeble and unresisting Negroes.

CHAPTER V.

THE same spirit animated the other troops, both volunteers and regular soldiers, who were marched to the eastern part of Jamaica, to assist in putting down the imaginary rebellion; and deeds were enacted, the bare recital of which awakens both shame and indignation. Some instances of these, taken at random from the evidence sworn to before the Royal Commissioners, will further serve to show how the black subjects of Her Majesty in Jamaica were dealt with, under the sanction of Governor Eyre, during the thirty days of martial law.

Rosa M'Bean left her husband on the 14th of October to go to Manchester market. On her way she met some soldiers, and they shot her. She was, however, not killed outright, and was taken home to her husband, to whom she related how she had been wounded. At the same time, and the same place, two men were wantonly killed, and another wounded, who, when the Commissioners were in the island, still lay in the hospital at Kingston.

Joshua Francis, an old black man, was sexton of a church at Monklands. When leaving the church on Tuesday, the 17th of October, he was walking along the highway with the keys in his hand, and was wantonly shot down by the soldiers, whom he was unfortunate enough to meet, and literally riddled with balls, these heroes having made a target of the poor old Negro. This was done without the slightest provocation. They also burned the house in which he lived with his daughter, and took away everything valuable they had in their possession. Some days afterwards the soldiers returned, and were about to burn a small house in which the daughter had taken refuge with her husband, who was sick. She entreated one of the officers to save it for the sake of her children; and on her telling him that she was the daughter of the slaughtered sexton, he gave orders that the house should not be destroyed.

Some Maroons went to Mill's River, to the house of a black man named Robert Bailey. His wife was standing at the door of the cottage, and the man who was leader of the party bade her " good evening," and inquired for her son, William Bailey. She said he was in the house, very sick with fever. The Maroons entered the house, and shot the sick youth as he lay upon his bed. They afterwards laid hands upon the father of the young man, and made him turn his face towards them, and then wantonly shot him down in the yard, with another man, named Robert Walker, who happened to be present. After this they set fire to the house, and then took their departure; carrying with them the clothes of the murdered men, and whatever else they chose to bear away.

At Harbour Head (Port Morant) some Maroons entered the house of John Noble, a black man. He was sick, and had been lying bed-ridden for many years. They directed him to get up and go out of the house. He said he could not, for he was not able. They then forced him out, tied him up to a tree, and shot him, leaving him there dead, and giving instructions that the body was to remain there and not to be buried. Briscoe, one of these ruffianly Maroons, who was identified with many acts of wanton cruelty and murder, and called himself *Captain Briscoe*, said, in his examination before the Commissioners, that the man was shot for the crime of having a son who was a rioter; and he pretended that he was a receiver of stolen goods.

Some black soldiers of the 1st West India Regiment laid hold of a man, named Sandy M'Pherson, near to Long Bay. They tied him, and were taking him along with them, a prisoner, when one of these savages levelled his musket and shot the poor fellow in the neck, and he fell dead. Another in the same village, who was hastening to get into his house when the white soldiers made their appearance, was caught by them, and shot in a similar way.

On the 17th of October, a black soldier belonging to the 1st West India Regiment, on his way from Man-. chioneal to Long Bay, met some constables with four black prisoners in their charge. He inquired what these men were, and being informed they were prisoners, he deliberately took them, one by one, and, placing them at a convenient distance, shot them all in detail. The same soldier had, a short time before, in sheer wanton-ness, shot a bull, the skeleton of which, picked clean by the vultures, lay upon the turnpike road when the Commissioners were carrying on their investigations. The soldier proceeded to Long Bay, where he found in the custody of a person named Berry six black prisoners suspected of stealing a sow, the property of one Christo-pher Codrington. The late manager of the Jamaica Cotton Company (then a justice of the peace) was present, with James Codrington, Mr. David Mayne, and several constables and assistants. In the presence of them all,—and such was the panic-stricken condition of the whole country, in consequence of the misrepresenta-tions of Governor Eyre, and the atrocious proceedings of the military authorities, that none dared to interpose by a word,—this single soldier was permitted to take these untried prisoners out, one by one, and put them to death by shooting them with his rifle, while the persons above named quietly stood by and looked upon the butchery. The widows of two of the victims, named Berry, appeared before the Royal Commissioners to give their dismal account of the tragedy which deprived them of their husbands. The next day after this brutal massacre had taken place, the sow the murdered men were supposed to have stolen, and for stealing which they had been put to death without any pretence of a trial, came out of the bush with a litter of young pigs, which sufficiently accounted for her disap-·pearance. Captain Hole, of the 2nd Battalion of the 6th Regiment, was informed soon after how these six innocent persons had been shot; but he seems to have made no effort to discover the murderer; nor was any attempt ever made to bring him to justice. It would have been perfectly easy to do so; for, the atrocious deed being perpetrated in the presence of numerous spectators, there could have been no difficulty in identifying the assassin.

On the 17th of October, another unfortunate was seized upon by one of the Codringtons at Long Bay. His name was Henry Dean; and the witness, who stated the facts on oath, thus spoke of the man's arrest:—"He went and hid himself in the bush because he had heard that the soldiers shot all the people, and he heard also that Mr. James Codrington had sent to take his wife, and his wife was big with child. He did not wish her to be hurt; so before they killed his wife, he came out to be killed instead; and as he came out, Mr. David Mayne ordered the constable to tie him. Mayne struck him across the face until his nose and mouth began to bleed. 'Man! man!' bawled the prisoner, 'what have I done to you?' He and two others were then tied behind a carriage, and compelled to run behind it to Manchioneal, and that was the last that was seen of Henry Dean by those who knew him." On turning to the list of those who were put to death at Manchioneal there is found in it the name of G. H. Dean.

David Burke was shot at Manchioneal. The soldiers ordered him to go before them, and point out rebels. "He was a big stout young man," said a witness, "and he walked quite lumber-like, and they cried, 'He is a rebel,' and shot him dead."

Andrew Clarke was shot in his own house at Manchioneal, under the following circumstances, as described by his widow:—"I was sitting with the baby, and I saw a black soldier approach. He said to Andrew Clarke, 'Where are all the men's goods you have? Please bring them out.' Clarke said, 'I have been sick for three months, and did not interfere.' The soldier then entered the house, and searched it, but found nothing. Three other soldiers then came in and another man with them, and I explained to them that it was John Murray's house. They then shot my husband, and he dropped on his side and bawled for mercy: the soldiers told me to take myself out, and I came out. One of them then said, 'Put another bullet into that fellow's head;' and they blew out his brains. Having done all this, they then burnt the house with fire they had brought from the kitchen."

There was residing at Airy Castle, between Port Morant and Bath, a respectable black man, named James Williams. He was a member of the Methodist Church, maintaining his family in much comfort by his industry, and represented to me by his minister, the Rev. W. C. Murray, who was intimately acquainted with him, as a man of superior intelligence and unblemished reputation. During all the excitement that followed the outbreak at Morant Bay, he kept to his

own house as much as possible, and refrained from
going abroad, that he might preserve himself and
family from the perils by which they were surrounded.
But no black man's life was safe in those days, whatever might be his character and position, especially in
that neighbourhood, where murder and rapine were
rampant. In the same village there was living another
person of the same name, James Williams, who had,
at some previous time, in some way not known, incurred
the enmity of the before-mentioned ruffianly Maroon,
who was intrusted with some petty command, and
suffered to assume the title of Captain Briscoe amongst
the demi-savages to whose ranks he belonged. This
was a favourable opportunity to gratify his vengeance
with impunity; and he selected several of the men
under his command, and sent them to wreak his malice
upon the object of his dislike. They went to the village,
and in answer to their inquiries were directed to the
house of the first-named James Williams, who was both
better known and more respected than his name-sake.
He was at once seized and bound, the wife and family
turned out of the house, and the place plundered of
whatever the ruffians chose to take. The house was then
set on fire, and burnt to the ground. The poor fellow,
who could hardly persuade himself that they were in
earnest, was, in spite of all remonstrances on his own
part, and the entreaties of his family, dragged away to
a marl-pit close at hand, and there ruthlessly shot to
death. Immediately afterwards, Briscoe appeared
upon the scene, and, on looking upon the mangled
bleeding corpse, discovered that they had taken and
put to death the wrong person. The men were at once
dispatched in search of the other James Williams, whom
they soon found, and dealt with in a similar way, putting
him to death with their rifles, turning his wife and

children from their home, and setting fire to their dwelling. On the 5th of May, this year, 1867, I was passing through the village of Airy Castle, on my way to conduct Divine service at Bath, when the driver of the vehicle in which I was travelling, pointing to a lovely spot embosomed in a rich grove of various fruit-trees, said, " There stood the house of James Williams," and, driving on a few rods further, he drew up the vehicle in front of a deep marl-pit by the side of the road, and, pointing his whip towards it, said, " There is the place where James Williams was shot by the Maroons, and I was there and saw it done." These atrocities were reported by Mr. Murray, the Wesleyan Minister at Bath, to Mr. Fyfe, the commander of the Maroons; but he made no attempt to have the murderers punished as they deserved. One beneficial result, however, followed Mr. Murray's interposition : Briscoe and his party, who had been sent to ravage and destroy through a wide extent of country, were recalled; and thus, doubtless, many innocent lives were saved, and many dwellings preserved from desolation; for every step of this ruthless band was marked by rapine and blood. Great care was required afterwards to guard Mr. Murray against the vengeance of these Maroons, who had been disappointed in their anticipated feast of blood and plunder.

It may not be out of place to remark here that the Maroons of Jamaica are not, as many suppose, the aborigines of the island, or their descendants. All the aboriginal inhabitants were exterminated by the Spaniards before the island became a British possession. When the Spainards surrendered the colony to the English, they left behind them a number of their African slaves, who, not caring to subject themselves to the will of new masters, betook themselves to the mountain fastnesses, and formed their own settlements where it was exceedingly difficult, from the impracticable nature of the ground, to get at them. With these Spanish slaves originated the body of people known as the Maroons of Jamaica, accessions being made to their number from time to time by runaway slaves escaping from English masters. Frequent collisions took place between them and the British authorities in the island; and at the latter end of the last century attempts were made by the Government to subjugate these Arabs of the mountains. It was with the greatest difficulty, and after a large sacrifice both of treasure and life, that this was accomplished; the Maroons resisting the attempt to invade their strongholds with much bravery, and repelling their assailants in many actions with great slaughter. On their submission, certain rights and privileges were conceded to them by treaty. During the continuance of slavery, these wild mountaineers were largely employed as a rural police, for the capture of fugitive slaves. A few of them have come under religious influence, and have attached themselves to Christian Churches in the neighbourhood of their mountain settlements; but, for the most part, they are an ignorant and savage race, far removed from civilization, and well suited to be actors in such cruel and sanguinary proceedings as those which disgraced Jamaica in 1865. Governor Eyre summoned them in large numbers to assist in putting down the imaginary rebellion; and let them loose, with other hungry dogs of war, against the unfortunate and unresisting Negroes. After working wide-spread desolation and bloodshed through the eastern part of the island, to the disgrace of the colony, they were fêted and honoured as if they had been the saviours of the country.

Dr. Morris and Lieutenant Cullen, of the 6th Regiment, were charged with the murder of three men near the iron bridge at Golden Grove. It was sworn by eye-witnesses that the three men were shot without trial, and one of them, not being quite dead, was dispatched by the revolver of one of the murderers. The bodies were buried on the spot; and after the accusation was made against these officers, they were exhumed, leaving no doubt whatever as to the substantial truth of the allegation that the men were put to death as the witnesses stated. The accused officers were tried by court-martial on this charge; but doubts were raised on some points, which furnished the opportunity for acquitting them. It is, however, beyond all question, that the three victims were brutally murdered by men calling themselves British officers.

In those evil days, Provost-marshal Ramsay distinguished himself by acts of brutality and ruffianism which have seldom been surpassed. He was understood to have been formerly connected with the army in some subordinate capacity; after which he became associated with the police establishment in Jamaica. For some reason unexplained, this individual was selected to fill the office of Provost-marshal during the reign of terror; and the villanies related concerning him would appear to be fabulous and incredible, if so many of them had not been proved on oath, by unexceptionable testimony, before the Royal Commissioners. On the 14th of October Ramsay made his appearance in the streets of Bath, very early in the morning, crying aloud, "Martial law is proclaimed. God save the Queen." An old soldier, named Peter Bruce, was appointed to act as Provost-marshal's assistant. Accompanied by a man named Kirkland, a local Magistrate, and his assistant Bruce, Ramsay at once directed his footsteps to the gaol, where a number of prisoners had been already assembled, having been brought in by the Maroons, and immediately proceeded to flog them, without trial, indiscriminately, and without any authority except his own. One after another, a considerable number of these unfortunate people were thrown upon the ground, and held down by several persons, while they were lacerated with the cat; Ramsay himself, as proved by the evidence of Kirkland before the Commissioners, flogging fifteen of them with his own hand. It was at this place that women, some of them in a state of pregnancy, were subjected to the lash by these monsters; and here, as proved by the testimony of Assistant Provost-marshal Bruce, because the ordinary instruments of cruelty inflicted torture insufficient to gratify their sanguinary propensities, though made of strong knotted cord, and capable of causing terrible punishment, strings of twisted piano wire were added, to render the sufferings of the victims more excruciating and terrible.

When Ramsay gave his orders for the flogging of the prisoners, Bruce made a cat according to the regimental style, with nine tails, and three knots on each tail; but that was not considered sufficiently effective, and he was ordered to make a cat of wire. They were made of cord and wire, mixed according to the taste of those who made them. The tails were not limited to nine, but amounted to sixteen or seventeen strands with wire around them, and the wire was often knotted so as to cut the skin. This was all proved on oath before the Royal Commissioners by the testimony of numerous witnesses; and some remnants of these instruments of torture, which had been overlooked when Colonel Fyfe got the others destroyed out of the way, were produced before the Commissioners. "Were the punishments very severe?" was a question asked of Bruce. His answer was, "O, very! I have seen amongst soldiers three hundred lashes in the army, but I never saw anything like this."

The evidence of Thomas Beckford, a butcher at Bath, gives a good idea of the horrors of the time:—

"Mr. Kirkland sent to say I must go and assist to flog the people. I said I didn't able to flog; I never did; it would be hard for me to flog and to be killing beef. He said, if I did not flog, I would get a hundred lashes. I was compelled, for the sword and gun of the Maroon were around me. It was about the middle of martial law. On Friday the 13th, the regiment came up from Kingston. On Monday I began to kill beef for the Maroons; and on Wednesday, October 18th, I flogged forty-nine people that day. I know that one, Alick Taylor, had one hundred lashes, and was hanged. George Tyrer had one hundred, William Burke had one hundred, Thomas Bolton had one hundred, Daniel Taylor had one hundred, Toby Butler had one hundred, and was hanged. All the rest had fifty, twenty-five, or thirty. Nobody helped me that day. All the females had sixteen lashes. I cannot tell exactly how many were women; about twenty. I think one Fanny Junor, who was heavy with child, had nineteen lashes. She said she was, and she was sent to be examined, and they said she was not. Married women examined her. She *was* big with child at that time. The female cat was like this,—a piece of knotted twine. Some had seventeen and some sixteen lashes strung with it, all with knots the same as this. The men were flogged with this cat (specimen produced). There were about sixteen or seventeen strands like that, all with wire round in that way, and all that length, put into a good piece of stick. I took that piece, and kept it since that time. My hand got tired with flogging, and I cried out, and they mixed a glass of rum and water to give me strength. Mr. Kirkland sent it to me. I began about nine in the morning, and I never left off till about four in the afternoon."

Amongst the victims at Bath were two persons, Jasper Hall Livingstone and his wife Cecilia, both of them members of the Wesleyan Church at that place, under the care of the Rev. W. C. Murray, the native Wesleyan Missionary then stationed there.   The man was put to death, after being brutally flogged; and the poor woman, although pregnant, was subjected to the torture of the cat, part of the punishment being inflicted with the diabolical instrument made of iron wire.   The only crime committed by them was knocking at the gate of a shop, where they were desirous of making some purchases.   The following is the substance of the evidence given by Mrs. Livingstone before the Commissioners :—

"I am the widow of Jasper Hall Livingstone.   On Thursday, the 13th of October, I told my husband I wanted something, and if he would carry me to Joe Williams' shop in Bath.   We went to the gate, and the gate was locked, and we asked if they would let us in.   The young man said he could not let us in to-day.   Joseph Williams afterwards pointed out my husband to Mr. Kirkland, and said he had attempted to break into the shop.   They took him to Mr. Kirkland's yard.   Joseph Williams said something against him.   He was ordered to have a hundred lashes.   I was there and saw it.   He fell off the cart to which he was tied. He fainted away.   Water was thrown upon him.   Mr. Kirkland ordered him to be sent to Morant Bay."   (In the list of those executed at Morant Bay is the name of Jasper Livingstone, October 27th, charged with plunder and rebellion; the fact of himself and wife knocking at the gate in open day, and before many witnesses, where they wished to purchase necessaries, being made to bear this construction.) "I was taken before Mr. Kirkland the same day as my husband was flogged.   The same Joseph Williams gave evidence against me.   I was tied to the cart.   They gave me twenty-six lashes. I was then in the family way. I did not tell them so. I am eight months now; I was four months then. I was flogged on the Friday, and they burned my house on the Saturday. The Maroons took from me three horses and a mare in foal. I have a large family."

Richard Harris, an intelligent black planter, who acted as constable during martial law, said in his evidence, " When they flogged Mrs. Livingstone, and gave her four or five lashes, and saw the wire cut her back, Bruce said, ' This cat won't do to flog the women; ' and they changed it, and sent upstairs to where Mr. Duffers was, and got another cat without wire, and gave her the balance of the lashes."

After inaugurating these horrible atrocities in the beautiful little village of Bath, Ramsay left them to be carried on by one of kindred spirit with himself, the man Kirkland, and returned to Morant Bay. Several prisoners were sent ashore from the " Wolverine " war steamer, and they were given into the custody of Ramsay; who, without waiting for any form of trial, set about to hang them at once, giving directions to several sailors how to adjust the ropes. One of these prisoners, who by some means escaped death, said, in giving his testimony before the Royal Commissioners, " We commenced to pray, at least I did, in my heart. I said, ' I do not know what I done, and I am going to be executed.' While this was going on, an officer happened to pass by, and said to Ramsay, ' What are you going to do with these people? ' Ramsay said, ' This lot has got to be hanged off first.' The officer said, ' Take them to the court-house first; ' and Ramsay pulled his beard and stamped his foot on the ground, but immediately marched us off to the court-house." This came before the Commissioners in the evidence of Richard Clarke.

That day three men and a woman were hanged by
Ramsay, who suspended them to the rails of the court-
house, the sailors pulling their feet and jerking them
until they were dead.

The same day, or the next, Ramsay shot a young
man in the most wanton and brutal manner, near the
village of White Horses, without trial or provocation of
any kind. His name was Archy Francis. He threatened also to shoot a man, named James Loague, for
merely looking at him. "You damned black brute,"
he said, "if you look at me again I will shoot you."

This unexampled ruffian proclaimed himself to the
poor ignorant people at White Horses *King of Jamaica,*
and threatened to shoot a woman who looked at him,
telling her he had shot a man at the waterfall. When
Ramsay and his companions had passed on, she went to
the waterfall, a short distance off, and found a boy,
named Henry Bunnyman, whom this Ramsay, with
some others, had shot, and left weltering in his blood.
In this cruel act he was assisted by some soldiers who
were in his company. The public road lay close to the
sea, and the youth was bathing in the shallow water
near the shore, when the assassins happened to pass by.
Ramsay, and those with him, thought it excellent fun
to make a target of him, and shoot at him in the water.
(The lad was fired at, amongst others, by a Lieutenant
O'Connor, a British officer, who ought to have all the
honour given to him of taking part in this unprovoked
murder of an unoffending lad. It must have been a
matter of no small surprise to the Commissioners that
amongst the officers of the British army were to be
found such unmitigated ruffians as some of those who
distinguished themselves by their sanguinary proceedings during these dark days.)

The following testimony was given by James Loague,

a blacksmith at White Horses, before the Royal Commissioners :—

"I remember the Saturday after the disturbances at Morant Bay. In the morning I heard that the soldiers were coming, and I put on my clean clothes and took a walk, and said, 'They will protect the innocent.' I met Lieutenant Oxley and Mr. Testard, and they were conversing about it. After leaving them I saw Inspector Ramsay on horseback, galloping up. He said, 'Who is that d—d black brute?' and rushed on me. By this time the marine sailors were below Mr. Enniss's house at White Horses, and I went down immediately as he said. He told me to fall into the rank, and I did so. After that we were all going up together, and when we came to Testard's shop, I saw, about ten yards from Donaldson's place, a young man named Archy Francis come out of a yard to meet them ; and Mr. Ramsay shot him in the head, and ordered that he was not to be buried, but must remain there, as an example to the rest. He left him there ; and as he shot him I looked upon him."—"Looked upon whom?" the Commissioners asked.—"Ramsay. He said, 'You d—d black brute, if you look at me again I will shoot you.' Archy Francis was about twenty or forty yards from Ramsay when he was shot."

Ramsay, when he perpetrated this wanton deed, had only a few minutes before committed the murder of Henry Bunnyman, having stopped behind his party to assassinate the unoffending lad. The following is the substance of the evidence given before the Commissioners by Sophia Bates, the mother of Henry Bunnyman by a former husband :—

"About five o'clock in the evening she saw her son crawling into the yard, covered with blood, and observed that he had been shot. He died on the Sunday night at nine o'clock. When he came in, the mother asked him how he came by his wounds, and he said, 'Mother, I went to take a bathe, and the soldiers came, and I ran to the sea-side and dived, and they shot at me, and don't catch me. When I rise, I look back, don't see anybody, and I come out;' and then, he said, a white man clapped his hand on his shoulder, and shot him right on the hip."

The mother in her evidence enters into some further details of what her son told her, from which it may be inferred that there were two persons present, one who had a horse, and one on foot; that after they had shot the boy, the one on horseback directed the other to finish him, and this seems to have been attempted with circumstances of horrid cruelty. After the boy had " stretched out," not able to bear any more, the one on horseback asked if he was dead, and, being so assured, rode off and left him. In addition to the wounds, when he crawled into his mother's yard his face was all chopped, as with a stone, and he was naked. Lieutenant O'Connor admits in his evidence, that a man was fired at before the party came to White Horses, and he was fired at by Lieutenant O'Connor himself. Apparently, however, Ramsay remained behind and watched for the boy coming ashore, when he supposed that the party who had been firing at him in the water had taken their departure, and deliberately murdered him. That Ramsay was behind the party is proved by the evidence of Loague, the blacksmith, already quoted, who explained that he came galloping up after the witness had met Lieutenant Oxley, and committed the second murder by shooting Archy Francis, as described in his testimony.

Ramsay made it a common practice, showing the delight he took in human suffering, to flog prisoners, in sheer wanton cruelty, who were condemned to be executed. And many a poor sufferer was dragged to the gallows with his person fearfully lacerated, and streaming with gore, from the brutality of this man. A gun, or gun-carriage, was brought out upon the square before the burnt court-house at Morant Bay, and the prisoners were tied up to the wheel, and flogged with the navy cat, by sailors belonging to Her Majesty's ship of war "Wolverine." One of Ramsay's numerous deeds of cruelty brought himself within the shadow of the gallows. It was distinctly proved by the sworn testimony of many witnesses, that while a poor fellow, named Marshall, was undergoing a cruel torture by the lash, he turned round in his agony, and cast a look at Ramsay, who was superintending the punishment, at the same time grinding his teeth either through pain or indignation. The cruel wretch observed this, and immediately ordered him to be taken down and hanged; and in a few moments the suffering man, his back streaming with blood, was writhing in the agonies of death upon the rail which was made to serve the purposes of a gallows. No offence had been proved or charged against him. The following testimony concerning this cruel act was given on oath by Mr. Lake :—

" On receiving the forty-seventh or forty-eighth lash, the man turned round and ground his teeth. The Provost-marshal ordered him to be hanged immediately. His back was like a bit of raw beef, bleeding very profusely. He was taken down, thrown on his back, his hands and feet tied, a rope put round his neck, and thrown over a rail; and then he was twisted up as you would a barrel of flour. He had no drop. After he had been suspended about three minutes, a huge white stone was taken and put between his arms, which were tied behind him. The Provost-marshal said, ' Take him from the gun, and hang him.' "

Mr. Daniel Marshalleck, of Morant Bay, a Magistrate, thus describes the scene :—

"I was sitting at my house, and I heard that a man was to be flogged. I went out in the parade, in company with another party, and I saw a man, by the name of Marshall, being tied; he was tied to a gun and flogged; he had a great number of lashes given to him, I think very nearly fifty; I did not count them, but there was a great number of lashes. The man shrieked a little, and drew up his body; and I heard the Provost-marshal, Mr. Ramsay, say, 'Take down that man and hang him.' The man was immediately taken down. He was so weak that he could scarcely walk; he was pulled along, and when got just under the hanging place he was pulled up; a rope was put round his neck as he was lying down, or very nearly so; he could scarcely stand, and he was pulled up and hanged just as a barrel would be hoisted up the side of a ship."

By direction of the Government, Ramsay was indicted for this murder; but a planter grand jury defeated all attempts to bring upon him the punishment such a crime deserved.

Amongst the troopers on duty at Morant Bay, was Mr. Joseph Gordon Smith, a nephew of George William Gordon. He describes what he witnessed :—

"Ramsay flogged the prisoners without even asking their names—nearly all, I believe; but I did not see all, because we were dismissed when a shower of rain came on. Afterwards I went to the guard-room, and he was then swearing five of them, with their hands fastened and a rope round their necks; and he was swearing them in these words: 'You shall well and truly state what G. W. Gordon has to do with the rebellion;' and between each part of this, a sailor came down with the whip over their shoulders. Mr. Lindo, the solicitor to this Commission, saw my face, and saw that I was very much excited; and he put his hand on my mouth and said, 'For God's sake, Smith, keep your mouth shut.' "

One of those apprehended by Ramsay at Morant Bay was a grey-haired, most respectable old Negro, named Chisholm, who kept a shop in the town. Mr. Gordon had been in the habit of baiting his horses at Chisholm's shop when travelling through Morant Bay; and occasionally corresponded with the old man on business and politics. This, of course, was sufficient to mark him out as a fit object for Ramsay's brutality. He gave this testimony before the Commissioners :—

"I keep a little shop at Morant Bay. I was taken in custody on October 16th, by Ramsay himself. He came in with Mr. Richard Cooke, who brought him there; he collared me, and I said, 'What do you want me for?' He hit me two blows. He took me to the police station; and I remained in custody, in the gaol in the workhouse, from October 16th to December 11th. I was never tried; I was flogged. Ramsay came into the prison one morning, and began asking me if Gordon had told the people that they were to kill buckra. I told him, 'No, Mr. Gordon never said such a thing.' Then they took a cat and gave it to a soldier; and the soldier put it on my back, put it on my back, and put it on my back [meaning three lashes], and then Ramsay cried, 'Stop!' I had only my shirt on my back. Then he asked me again the same question; and I said, 'Mr. Gordon never did, he never did, he was a peace-maker.' Then he said, 'You are a liar!' and he struck me on my face with his fist, and the soldier struck me with a stick; they flogged me with a whip and stick both. Ramsay took a loaded pistol to blow out my brains. By striking me, the blood was made to flow, and it washed over my face; and though there was some person in the gaol besides Ramsay and the soldier, I could not see. I do not know whether General Nelson was present when

I was struck. My head was scattered, and the blood was washing me. After that he saw the blood, and asked me where I got it. They took up Mrs. Chisholm, and Eliza my grandchild, and a little child. We were all in gaol, and nobody was at my house, and the money and things were taken away by the people."

On Wednesday, October 18th, Ramsay made a flying visit to Stoney Gut, to proclaim martial law, accompanied by two policemen; and shortly afterwards a party of soldiers arrived there, under Lieutenant Oxley; so that "Stoney Gut," "the great stronghold of the rebels," as it was absurdly called, to give something like colour to the idea that the outbreak was "*a rebellion*," was actually taken by Ramsay, with his cat in his belt, and two policemen. A man of the name of Levinston, alarmed at the approach of the troops, rushed out of his house, and attempted to escape. He was shot at and wounded, but escaped with his life. His wife was seized by Ramsay, and thrown down upon her face, and flogged by the policemen on the lower part of her person, to compel her to tell where Paul Bogle was. She said she did not know; and the flogging was repeated on three successive occasions, twenty-five lashes being given each time. She was then taken as a prisoner to Paul Bogle's chapel, where the sailors and marines were, and Ramsay took the rope of the lamp of the chapel, and put it round her neck, and threatened to hang her if she did not tell where Bogle was. The woman states that she was raised off the ground, and that she felt her eyes begin to start out of her head. Lieutenant O'Connor admits the rope was round her neck from four to six minutes. A very worthy and gallant officer and gentleman he must be, to stand by and suffer a woman to be thus treated under his command! He also admits that the rope was "just tightened," but denies that it could affect the face or her powers of breathing. But it is probable the sufferer understood what she felt better than this gallant ornament of the British army. She was afterwards tied outside the chapel "like a beast," as a policeman phrased it, and kept outside all night, while the men were inside.

Ramsay attempted to hang two men from the Airy Castle district, named M'Queen and Mitchell, without trial and without authority; but he was prevented by Lieutenant De Worgan, of the "Wolverine," who interposed, and declared that he would suffer no man to be punished without trial where he commanded. Another British officer, an Ensign of the 6th Regiment, showed a very different spirit. He was content to act as assistant hangman under Ramsay; and had actually, with others assisting, proceeded so far as to put ropes around the necks of the intended victims, and put them up on barrels to be turned off, when De Worgan interfered, and prevented the consummation of the murder. All honour to Lieutenant De Worgan, who dared to be just and humane when terror and cruelty reigned all around !

It was Ramsay's practice to extort evidence by torture and flogging against the prisoners he wished to bring to the gallows. A Wesleyan Missionary had occasion to call at the police station at Morant Bay, and became an eye-witness of the fact. While he was there a man was tied up to be flogged. After he had received several lashes, the question was put to him whether he had taken any oath to join the rebels? He said, " No." "Until you tell us the truth we will flog you," was the rejoinder of Ramsay; and the lash was vigorously applied again. This process was continued until the poor fellow, to escape from their tortures, at length gave the answer that was desired ; and then the punishment was continued until he made the further admission, that Paul Bogle was the man who administered the oath to him. On evidence thus obtained by torture, victims were sentenced to the gallows.

The atrocities committed by this man Ramsay would fill a volume. He revelled in tyranny and cruelty, until his very name became a terror. A young man, for speaking to another person near the police station, was tied to a column and flogged by Ramsay's order. To one Richard Clarke, for daring to speak to him, he ordered fifty lashes to be administered, which he afterwards reduced to twenty-five. He flogged one of the volunteers for speaking under the window of his room; and when, at the suggestion of the police sergeant, the man begged to be let off, he ordered that another dozen should be inflicted. The man's name was Edward Gentle. Men were ordered to be flogged by Ramsay for winking, not taking off their hats, &c. A poor fellow was going to the gallows, tied and bound for the slaughter, when his little boy handed him a hat, to shield his naked head from the rays of the sun. Ramsay happened to see it, and rewarded the filial act of the boy with fifty lashes; and while the father was being brutally strangled, with other sufferers, the poor lad, tied to a gun close at hand, was groaning and bleeding under the lash. Several coloured Ministers of religion were amongst the prisoners arrested by Governor Eyre's orders, and sent on to Morant Bay, to be tried and put to death, because some months before they had, in the exercise of their rights as British subjects, taken part in public meetings at which his own administration was not always spoken of in flattering terms. These men were marched out, under the orders of Ramsay, day after day, and compelled to look on while the Negroes were butchered, eighteen or twenty at a time, and others cruelly flogged. One of these coloured Ministers, who had been selected for the slaughter, and kept a prisoner for several weeks, told me that he always kept his eyes turned away from Ramsay when he was near, not daring to look upon him, lest he should resent it as an offence, and order him out to be flogged. "How dare you look at me?" said he to a poor trembling creature, whose look had been fixed upon him with the sort of fascination with which men sometimes regard a horrid monster. "Take him out, and give him a dozen!" It was thus that this man was suffered and, indeed, authorized by Governor Eyre to treat the free subjects of Queen Victoria in 1865.

CHAPTER VI.

THE case of Mr. George William Gordon has received a large degree of public attention, as standing out prominently amongst the horrors and atrocities which mark the period of Mr. Eyre's administration in Jamaica. Many attempts have been made to misrepresent the character of Mr. Gordon. Governor Eyre himself, with lamentable disregard to truth, has not scrupled to give utterance to slanders against his victim, which have called forth a triumphant refutation from Christian Ministers and others intimately acquainted with his character and history, whose honest indignation was aroused by this wicked attempt of ex-Governor Eyre to blacken the character of the innocent man whom he had hurried to an ignominious death.

The following letter from Mrs. Gordon appeared in "The Times" of April 6th, 1867:—

"TO THE EDITOR OF 'THE TIMES.'

"SIR,—Your report of the recent proceedings at Market Drayton gives special prominence to certain statements touching the character of my late husband, G. W. Gordon. I did not wish to become his vindicator, feeling assured that time would do him justice; but I am urged by many friends, whose entreaties I can no longer resist, to protest against those assertions as utterly false and calumnious.

"As the widow of a man who was wrongfully put to death, I ask at your hands the insertion of this protest from me; and I would request the additional favour of your publishing the subjoined testimonial to his character, signed by persons whose reputation for integrity has never been questioned.

"'In a dispatch from Mr. Eyre to Mr. Cardwell, dated King's House, January, 1866, to be found in the Blue Book on the Jamaica disturbances, entitled, 'Papers laid before the Royal Commission of Inquiry by Governor Eyre,' the following paragraph appears at p. 196, par. 4:—

"'It is well known out here that Mr. Gordon was universally regarded as a bad man, in every sense of the word; reported to be grossly immoral, and an adulterer, a liar, a swindler, dishonest, cruel, vindictive, and a hypocrite. Such are the terms applied to the late G. W. Gordon; and I believe abundant proof might be adduced of all these traits.'

"'The undersigned, having resided in the island many years, and having had very considerable opportunities of knowing and forming an estimate of the late Mr. Gordon's character in his various relations, do hereby protest against the foregoing allegations as made by Mr. Eyre, and declare them to be totally without foundation.

"'(Signed) James Phillippo, sen., Baptist Missionary, Jamaica; William Andrews, attorney-at-law, Kingston, Jamaica; Robert Osborn; James Bell; Alexander Fiddes, F.R.C.S. Edin.; Andrew Lyon, Common Councilman of the city and parish of Kingston; Thomas Geddes, Missionary, Savanna-la-Mar; James Scott, M.R.C.S. Eng.: Abraham Pinto, merchant; Mr. Ramos, merchant; Robert Gordon, priest of the Church of England, head-master of Wolmer's Grammar School, Kingston.'

"One of my greatest consolations in my present state of bereavement is my conviction of my husband's innocence, and of the thorough uprightness of his character, and that one day these will be fully established.

"I am, Sir, yours obediently,

"M. GORDON."

"*Watford, Herts, April 5th.*"

That Mr. Gordon was not a common man may be inferred from the fact that, from the condition of a slave, he raised himself to a respectable position in colonial society; and, while yet a comparatively young man, obtained a place in the Legislature, of which he continued to be a member until his tragic death. That he was not the bad man Mr. Eyre describes, is proved by the testimony already given in the preceding pages by the Rev. Dr. King and Dr. Fiddes, both of whom had the best opportunities of knowing him as a man, and also as a Christian. The touching vindication of the slandered martyr by his mourning widow speaks for itself. A member of the Jamaica House of Assembly, who differed with Mr. Gordon on public measures, gives an account of him very different from that of Mr. Eyre, and places the ex-Governor's veracity in a very questionable light :—

"The Jamaica House of Assembly has been for the last twenty years a planters' assembly, where wrongs were heaped like Pelion on Ossa. It has brought destruction on its own head; and many good men who were members of it must rejoice over its fall. Mr. Gordon had been, in better times, a member of the House; and in later days, when corruption was rampant, he found time to resume his labours there; and I am bound in the cause of truth and fairness to state that, though disagreeing in many things with him, and disliking his offensive allusions to Mr. Eyre, he was one of the few really useful men in the House. Indeed, from his peculiar amiability of disposition, his courage, and reliance on what he would call 'the good cause,' he constituted a very host in himself. Month after month he was seen to neglect his own affairs, and give himself up to the people's cause. 'The poor people of Jamaica are oppressed by vile laws!' was his incessant cry; and whether the idea was an idle dream, springing from a morbid mind, or a fact which was undeniable, Mr. Gordon spoke with amazing seriousness ; and he sometimes commanded, as I think he always deserved, admiration for his heroic defence of the rights of the poorer classes, and of the just claims of humanity."

"Mr. Gordon," says a lady who knew him well, "was a benevolent and just man, who had incurred the resentment of the planter class and of certain officials, by his exposure of abuses, and his unwavering fidelity to the cause of the coloured people. Mr. Gordon was one of the best of men; intelligent, kind-hearted, active in all measures for the amelioration of the condition of the poor, and honourably known for the stand he made against the oppressions of the governing class."

The Rev. Edwin Blake, Wesleyan Minister, who was well acquainted with Mr. Gordon, both as to his public life and private character, says,—

[Scotland]

"He was a member of the Church of England, but took the chair at Wesleyan or Baptist Missionary meetings. He was a man of extensive information, of most generous impulses ; and he had laboured long to promote the welfare of his fellow-creatures. He was thoroughly devoted to God, and concerned himself sincerely in promoting the welfare of those around him. He was most liberal in his contributions to the cause of God in every department. There was scarcely a chapel that required building, a school established, or any good work carried on, that did not find a hearty supporter in G. W. Gordon."

Mr. Gordon became a martyr to the fidelity with which he laboured for the interests of the down-trodden labourers of Jamaica, misgoverned and plundered by those above them. If, like some others around him, he had in public life looked chiefly to his own interests and sought his own aggrandisement, with his fearless

energy of character he might have acquired ease, and
honour, and office with its emoluments, and escaped
the melancholy fate that unhappily overtook him. But,
with disinterested regard to the poor and lowly, he stood
forward to advocate their cause in the face of abundant
obloquy and scorn, fully aware of the resentment with
which his proceedings were regarded by his political
opponents, and the intense malignity cherished towards
him by Governor Eyre and his adherents. On the 10th
of May, 1865, only a few months before he was put to
death, he wrote to Mr. Chamerovzow with almost pro-
phetic truth :—

"I have to contend with hatred and persecution of no
ordinary kind at present. You will, by a paper sent to you,
see that the government, judge, attorney-general, and
special jury, are all conspired against me here; and I believe, if some of them found the opportunity, they would
unscrupulously dispatch me. But the Lord is with us,
and the God of Jacob has promised to be our refuge, and
our present help in trouble."

That opportunity arose with the outbreak at Morant
Bay; and, as Mr. Gordon had predicted, his political
opponents eagerly seized upon it, and "unscrupulously
dispatched him." The whole circumstances of his
trial and death, taken with the antecedents, mark the
case as one of the foulest murders on record; and the
solemn and elaborate charge of the Lord Chief Justice
Cockburn, delivered to the grand jury on the indictment of Messrs. Nelson and Brand, stamps this character upon the transaction.

"During the thirty days' continuance of martial law in
four of the adjacent parishes," writes Dr. Fiddes, "Kingston

bore every impress of a city suffering under a reign of terror: anxiety was depicted on every face. I had no dread or fear of any general rising of the Negroes; for I always doubted the probability of such an occurrence. But I did feel alarm at seeing a man working the state machine, and wielding all the power and authority vested in him by right of his office, whom I considered to be influenced by apparitions of sedition and high treason which really had no existence, except in his own imagination; and I was doubly alarmed from a knowledge of the fact that he was principally advised and counselled by Dr. Bowerbank, who, it is notorious, saw a lion in every path, and a grinning skeleton in every compartment of the state. Arrests were being daily made of persons having no complicity in any rebellious movement, and who had never interfered directly or indirectly in such unlawful matters."

Governor Eyre had, at Port Morant, on the 14th of October, three days after the outbreak, as we have described, been present, and taken an active part in the immolation of the first victim of martial law. Thence he went to Morant Bay, and embarked for Port Antonio; more victims being offered at both places. On the 17th he returned in the " Wolverine " ship of war to Kingston, bent, as results show, upon availing himself of the opportunity now offered to effect the destruction of his formidable political opponent, G. W. Gordon. Without the loss of a moment, apparently, he issues a warrant for the apprehension of Gordon, and a diligent search is immediately set on foot for the destined victim. At first he could not be found; but, hearing that a warrant had been issued to apprehend him, on the advice of his friend Dr. Fiddes, Mr. Gordon went to the house of General O'Connor, the Commander of the forces, to place himself at the disposal of the authorities. While he was there, Governor Eyre came in,

7

accompanied by Dr. Bowerbank, and no sooner set eyes on Mr. Gordon than he hastily stepped up to him, and, invading the office of the policeman, apprehended Mr. Gordon as his prisoner. So eager was this representative of Her Majesty to complete the sacrifice of his opponent, that, barely permitting him to take a last hasty farewell of his wife, to whom he was fondly attached, within half an hour from the time of his arrest he was on the way to the scene of slaughter. When he entered the house, he said to Mrs. Gordon, " I am to be taken to Morant Bay at once, to die this evening." He then handed her his watch, with his purse ; and with one last embrace, one final farewell, which was all that was permitted to him, he parted from his wife, only to meet her again in the better land. The steam of the " Wolverine " was already up, and in an incredibly short time—contrasting very remarkably with the want of promptitude in despatching the same steamer with troops a week before—Governor Eyre, like a ravenous bird with its prey in its clutch, was speeding away with his victim to Morant Bay : " at which place," says Dr. Fiddes, " the functions of the court-martial were being exercised so heartily and with so much glee, and the work of flogging and of hanging was so diligently performed, that it actually seemed as if the inmates of Pandemonium had left their dwelling-place and come to earth for the purpose of scourging frail humanity. From what I saw of the manner of Mr. Gordon's seizure, and from his immediate transference from a place where no martial law existed to a town where it was in full activity, I concluded that his fate was sealed."

When Mr. Gordon was taken on board the " Wolverine," men shook their heads, and declared that " his life was not worth a pin, *for Mr. Eyre was his keeper ;* " and a member of the Executive Committee was heard to say that, "if he had twenty necks, they would all be broken." A malefactor condemned for the foulest crime could not have been treated with more cruelty and vindictiveness than this unfortunate gentleman. He was shackled, and fed upon biscuits and water; no one being permitted to speak to him, except those who heaped reproaches and curses upon his head.

He was as yet untried, and against him, as afterwards appeared, nothing but perjured testimony and the flimsiest allegations could be brought; but he was at once treated as if he had been a convicted murderer. All this time he was in the custody of Mr. Eyre himself, who took him to Morant Bay and delivered him in person into the hands of those who were to put him to death. This inhumanity towards a helpless prisoner, apart from all the other circumstances of the case, would be in itself sufficient to cover Mr. Eyre with shame, and serves to illustrate the bad feelings by which he was actuated through the whole of the disgraceful tragedy.

A rough sea prevented the "Wolverine" from going into Morant Bay that evening, and she steamed away with the Governor and his prisoner on board to Port Antonio; so that it was not until the morning of the 20th of October that Mr. Gordon was landed. "On arriving at Morant Bay," says a member of the Assembly, "he was mobbed by the sailors, his shirt was pulled over his pantaloons, and he was jeered and laughed at by officers and men of the British navy."

That the army might not be behind the navy in brutality, one of the soldiers tore off Mr. Gordon's coat and waistcoat; another robbed him of his spectacles. And all this was done with the approbation of one at least of the officers; for Captain Ford, relating these incidents, says, "So you see that he was very little differently treated from the common herd." Sick, emaciated, con-

sumptive, and without coat or waistcoat, he was kept
standing in the sun for a long time.

Mr. Gordon spoke a few words to a man named
Clive, a fellow prisoner, who was next to him, when
Ramsay strode up, and threatened him with instant
death if he spoke. Mr. Gordon at length grew faint,
and sank upon the ground, his manacled hands pre-
venting him from helping himself. The sentry took
him, and allowed him to sit upon a stone. "Where is
that ——?" roared the Provost-marshal. "Who
told him to sit down?" The sentry explained that he
had sunk in a fainting state to the ground, and Ramsay
then directed his hands to be loosened a little. An
officer, in the course of the day, went to Ramsay, and
said to him, "If you do not take better care of Gordon,
you will not have the pleasure of seeing him hanged;
for he will die." The system adopted by Ramsay, of
compelling the untried prisoners to witness the daily
executions, and to dig the graves of the slaughtered, is
something new in the annals of torture. Mr. Gordon
was compelled thus to witness these scenes of horror
before he himself was martyred, Ramsay and some of
the officers taunting him with the certainty of his own
approaching doom. On one occasion he was led out
in front of all the other prisoners, when one named
William Grant was being put to death. Ramsay led
him forward, and, brutally directing his attention to the
contorted features of the struggling and dying man, as
he hung with his feet nearly touching the ground, said,
"See what he has come to, and to that you will certainly come." Mr. Gordon, with that meekness which
even his political opponents admit to have been one of
his characteristics, only bowed, and was led back to his
place. In his prison—a vile place, reeking with filth
and vermin—he was treated like a wild beast, and wor-

ried on every side. His prayers were ridiculed; and, but for the kindly interposition of Sergeant M'Kenzie, of the police force, his Bible would have been taken away from him.

In this filthy place he was kept during Friday, October 20th, and on Saturday was given up to the tender mercies of the court-martial, which was convened to give the colour of a judicial proceeding to the work of wholesale slaughter. If ever a man was foredoomed, Mr. Gordon was; a fact perfectly understood by his friends, who were aware that there was as little chance of his escaping the grip of the deadly foe into whose power he had fallen, as if he had been in the jaws of a wild beast. There was no martial law in Kingston, where Mr. Gordon was arrested by the hands of Governor Eyre; and there he could have been proceeded against in the ordinary administration of justice, if he had in any way violated the law. This was, however, too slow and uncertain a process for the purposes of Mr. Eyre, who, as results showed, had no reason whatever to charge Mr. Gordon with having been concerned in the riot, either directly or indirectly, or of being privy to it. Mr. Gordon had, however, incurred the deadly enmity of those who now revelled in the exercise of irresponsible power, and nothing less than his death would satisfy them. To make sure of this, and setting at defiance all law, and all humanity and justice, the victim is dragged, bound and helpless, to Morant Bay, where law, humanity, and justice are alike in abeyance.

General Nelson and Lieutenant Brand had already received from their chief something like a training in the work of slaughter; for both these men were present and active, when Fleming, the first sufferer subjected to the tender mercies of martial law, was put to death at Port Morant; and into the hands of these two

Mr. Gordon was consigned, while Mr. Eyre betook himself elsewhere to await the inevitable result. Under the direction of Nelson a court was formed, and at the head of it, as president, was placed the same Brand who had acted as hangman in the case of Fleming and finished that revolting act of cruelty with his revolver, who had been heard to declare, in the foul language of the lowest blackguardism, that "nothing would give him greater pleasure than to hang that damned son of a ——, Gordon." The other members of this court were a naval lieutenant named Errington, whose commission was four years old only; and Ensign Kelly, of one of the West India regiments, whose commission was not a year old. To this trio of young men, General Nelson handed over the prisoner, giving them a draught charge and *précis* of evidence. Nelson had been in close communication with Governor Eyre on board the "Wolverine," and perfectly understood his views. He had seen Mr. Gordon, though ill and untried, shackled and fed on biscuits and water, as if he had been a convicted felon, and perfectly acquiesced with the Governor and others in all this cruel injustice. There is very little room to doubt that the sentence to be pronounced was perfectly understood by the parties concerned, before a single witness was called into court. It is stated that Ramsay, the Provost-marshal, entered the prison yard that morning, and in presence of all the poor crouching miserables there, tried and untried, openly proclaimed that if any one would give evidence against Mr. Gordon, he would not only save his life, but be rewarded by the Government. The two witnesses who spoke against Mr. Gordon were those who responded to this invitation.

Into the details of this mockery of a trial we cannot enter. Before this court, composed of wild, harum-scarum young men, two of whom had been acting as assistant hangmen and had become fearfully familiar with the killing of men in cold blood, Mr. Gordon was brought to defend himself against charges of treason and rebellion, on October 21st. He had no intimation given to him of any specific acts laid to his charge; was allowed no time to prepare his defence; had no legal adviser; was not allowed to call any witnesses to repel the accusations made against him; and had to extemporize such defence as he was permitted to make, when he was exhausted by ill treatment, and both physically and mentally unfitted for the terrible crisis he was called to pass through.

One significant fact, which reflects undying shame upon General Nelson, and shows the heartless cruelty with which the fate of Gordon was pre-determined, was the suppression of a letter written by a legal friend and adviser of Gordon, and intended to assist him in his trial. Mr. William Wemyss Anderson, solicitor and clerk of the peace for Portland, a personal friend of Mr. Gordon, sought an interview with his former client on board the " Wolverine," which was not permitted. He then addressed a letter to him; and enclosed it under cover to General Nelson, who, to his everlasting disgrace, suppressed and destroyed it, so that it never reached the hands of its rightful owner. The following is a copy of this important communication :—

" TITCHFIELD, *October*, 1865.

" MY DEAR GORDON,

" HAVING been prohibited communication with you on board the 'Wolverine,' I have requested the favour of the General to forward this. I know nothing of the charges against you; but, as an old friend and professional adviser, I cannot refrain from tendering to you my advice, assuming that, whatever your errors may have been, they were committed before the proclamation of martial law. I advise you to plead :—

"First. That, on that account, you are amenable only to the ordinary civil and criminal courts of the country ; and,

"Second. That only is crime which is prompted by criminal intention ; and that you, having no such intention, are not criminally liable for the consequences, however disastrous these unhappily may have been.

"I need not add one word to assure you of my deepest sympathy ; but on such a topic it would be out of place now to enlarge.

"Yours very truly,

"W. WEMYSS ANDERSON."

General Nelson, when questioned before the Royal Commissioners, admitted having received that letter; and added, "I either tore it up at once, or gave it to my *aide-de-camp* to tear it up. It was not given to Mr. Gordon. I read it before it was destroyed."

Surely the suppression, under such circumstances, of a letter of such a character, and so important to the accused, was conduct so unbecoming a British officer and a gentleman, that it ought, if the military authorities of the country had done their duty, to have caused General Nelson's immediate dismissal from Her Majesty's service, as it is a mean and dastardly act which every upright and humane person must regard with the strongest reprobation. General Nelson was evidently afraid to let the unfortunate gentleman have the advantage of his solicitor's counsel, lest it should interfere with the nefarious doings which brought Mr. Gordon to an ignominious death. Probably it was this very letter that opened the eyes of General Nelson to the illegality of trying and executing civilians, by martial law, for alleged offences committed weeks and months before martial law was proclaimed; and so prevented the putting to death of Mr. Levien, Dr. Bruce, Mr. Phillips, and many others, who had been sent to Morant Bay to be dealt with in the same manner as Mr. Gordon.

The evidence adduced against Mr. Gordon proved literally nothing to substantiate the charges on which he was arraigned; and only in a case where the doom of the accused had been already decided upon, would it have been received as sufficient to justify his condemnation. Lord Chief Justice Cockburn says, in his charge to the grand jury, in the case of General Nelson and Lieutenant Brand, when these gentlemen were indicted for the murder of Mr. Gordon, "I cannot withhold from your attention the extraordinary character of the evidence, and the inconclusiveness and moral worthlessness of the evidence upon which Mr. Gordon was convicted. I have before me a record of the proceedings, and the charge which was then made against Mr. Gordon." His Lordship here proceeded with a lengthened and luminous review of the evidence which has appeared in the Royal Commissioners' Blue Book. He severely commented on the incomplete character of some portion of the evidence, remarking that it was " all moonshine to ground a charge of high treason upon such evidence." His Lordship then continued:— " I must particularly find fault with the taking of depositions of certain living persons who could have been called as witnesses. Contrary alike to the practice and justice of English law, these depositions have been put in as evidence when themselves could have been called. There cannot be the slightest doubt, according to all the rules of law, military or ordinary, that the great bulk of the evidence on which Mr. Gordon was convicted was legally inadmissible."

His Lordship further says:—

"No doubt, in the result, many lamentable circumstances have taken place. A man has been condemned and sentenced to death and executed on evidence which would not have been admitted before any properly constituted tribunal, and upon evidence which fails altogether to establish the crime with which he was charged, and of which he was convicted. He was a man obnoxious to the authorities; he was in the habit of reviling their jurisdiction, and calling it in question. He kept the minds of the population in a perpetual agitation by the power he exercised over them. He was a man of whom, in the opinion of the authorities, it was undoubtedly desirable to get rid: but they would not be justified in putting him to death, unless there was evidence that he was guilty of the crime laid to his charge. Intention is, at all times, the essence of crimes. I have seen it written, and I confess I shuddered as I read it, that it was justifiable to send Mr. Gordon to a court-martial to be tried, because a court-martial might be justified in convicting a man because he was mischievous. If that was the principle on which they proceeded in Mr. Gordon's case, I say it is one of the most lamentable instances of the miscarriage of justice with which history can furnish us."

"I cannot help thinking," says Chief Justice Cockburn, —"and I have a strong opinion on the point,—that the whole proceeding of taking Mr. Gordon from where he was, putting him on board a war steamer, and conveying him to Morant Bay, was an unjustifiable proceeding; and to Mr. Gordon it made the difference of life and death. I say so advisedly; because, after most careful perusal of the evidence produced against him, I am irresistibly led to this conclusion. If the man, upon that evidence, had been tried, —I am wrong: he could not have been tried on the evidence by an ordinary tribunal, presided over by any competent judge: I must stop myself,—I was going a great deal too far to say that he could have been tried on that evidence. He could not have been tried, because it would not be received. Three-fourths, nay, nine-tenths of the evidence upon which he was convicted and sentenced to death, is evidence that, according to rules, not only of ordinary law, but of military law, according to no rules of right and justice could have been admitted; would never have been admitted if a competent judge had presided; and if there had been a man of military experience of courts-martial, and who knew what rules ought to govern and regulate the reception of evidence. I should add that, not only that upon looking upon this evidence I come to this conclusion, but that no jury, however influenced by prejudice or passion, if guided by a competent, honest judge, could, upon evidence so morally and intrinsically worthless, and upon evidence so utterly inconclusive, have condemned that man upon a charge of murder. But then it is a very difficult question indeed, when you come to deal with the parties now charged before you on this indictment; and it is a very different thing to say they ought to be held responsible for what may have been the utterly illegal and unwarrantable act of the Governor and Custos in conveying Mr. Gordon to Morant Bay. I know it has been said and written, it was justifiable to take Mr. Gordon to Morant Bay, because he had been as much guilty of high treason and sedition there as at Kingston; and therefore, as his crime was local, it was competent to take him to trial in that part of the island where he was guilty of the charge. It is perfectly true crime is local; and a man must be tried where the offence is alleged to have been committed; but you have no right to choose your tribunal, or to say you will take a man to be tried at any particular place, because there may be a sterner judge there, or a better chance of obtaining a conviction than you would have in any other county. So that, although Mr. Gordon could be tried at Kingston, or at Morant Bay, when they had him at Kingston, I apprehend they ought to have tried him there. It is the principal town in the island; it has its assizes and courts of law; it is the place where the justices administer the law; it is in the county of Surrey, the county in which Morant Bay is situated, and the county in which the offence is alleged to have been committed. Therefore Mr. Gordon ought to have been tried at Kingston. But when Mr. Gordon was brought within martial law, assuming there was such a condition, it was not for the tribunal to inquire how he came among them. If Mr. Gordon had lived, and was subject to some minor punishment in Jamaica, and, having come to England, brought an action for damages against Mr. Eyre, it may well be that an English jury, presided over by an English judge, would have awarded him exemplary damages for the wrong that had been done him."

In this important charge, in which the Lord Chief Justice has shown that the whole proceedings in Mr. Gordon's case involved an outrage against all law and justice, he especially condemns the constitution of the court that tried and condemned him as anomalous and illegal, therefore possessing no lawful jurisdiction. After showing most lucidly and decisively that there is neither authority nor precedent for applying martial law . to civilians, as was done in Jamaica, he proceeds thus :—

"But now there is another serious question arises : that is to say, supposing that the true conclusion of the discussion is, that martial law is not the wild and extravagant exercise of authority which modern writers describe it to be; if martial law—simply a military law—is applied to civilians, then comes the question as to the constitution of this tribunal. If this tribunal was to be constituted according to military law, it was a bad tribunal, and had no jurisdiction. There is nothing in the Acts relating to the military service, and nothing in the Articles of War, which authorizes the mixing up of a court-martial with officers of the two services, and of which this court-martial was composed. According to the Acts of Parliament and the Articles of War applicable to the two services, no naval officer was entitled to sit on a

military court-martial, unless by express authority; and if
this be treated as a naval court-martial, it is equally illegal,
because it was not presided over by naval officers."

Thus, according to the decision of the highest legal
functionary in the realm, Mr. Gordon's trial and death
were, from beginning to end, stamped with the character
of a legal murder. His arrest by the hands of Governor
Eyre was an illegal act, inasmuch as it compromised the
dignity of the latter as Her Majesty's representative; his
removal to a district under martial law, in order that he
might there be tried and put to death, was illegal, and apparently prompted by the worst motives; the constitution
of the court that tried and condemned him was illegal,
so as to deprive it of all jurisdiction; and the evidence
on which the victim was condemned and executed was
" so morally and intrinsically worthless that no competent judge could have allowed it to be received." But
Mr. Gordon must be sacrificed; and, accordingly, he
was got rid of by as atrocious an outrage against the
liberty and lives of British subjects as the history of
modern times can furnish.

The circumstances attendant upon his execution were
in character with those of his arrest and trial, exhibit-
ing a degree of heartless barbarity most disgraceful to
British officers. No decision was pronounced by the
court, so as to afford an intimation to the prisoner of
the fate awaiting him; and Mr. Gordon was conducted
back to his wretched prison in ignorance of what was to
be the result of the mock trial to which he had been
subjected; though it could not have been difficult for
him to guess at it, from all that had taken place. The
death of the prisoner had, however, been resolved upon,
and no time was lost. The Governor was anxiously awaiting, at the seat of government, tidings of the issue of

the proceedings. *Death* is the sentence that has been agreed upon ; and, of course, it is immediately confirmed by Mr. Eyre. On Saturday Mr. Gordon has been tried; but all day on the Sabbath he is left in ignorance of what is impending, until Monday morning, when General Nelson waits upon him in his cell, quite early, to inform him that in one hour he is to die. This single hour is devoted to writing a letter to his wife, which has been permitted to appear in print, and is strikingly illustrative of the character of the man, and not unworthy the age of the martyrs. Simple and touching, expressive of a firm and unshaken reliance upon God, and breathing nothing but submission and the purest spirit of forgiveness towards his persecutors and murderers, it has appealed with resistless power to thousands of hearts against the cruelty and wickedness by which such a man was hunted to the grave. It is a complete refutation of the slanders penned by Governor Eyre against the murdered man, after he had gone to his dishonoured grave; for no man who was such as Mr. Eyre represented Mr. Gordon to have been could have written such a letter at such a time.

A minister of religion, living at Morant Bay, whose residence overlooks at some distance the ruins of the court-house, told me, as we sat gazing with melancholy interest upon the scene of the tragedy, "We all supposed, from the fact that no decision of the court-martial in the case of Mr. Gordon had been pronounced, that the trial was not finished, and would be resumed on the Monday morning, and an opportunity given to Mr. Gordon to make his defence; but, about eight o'clock, happening to look from the front of my residence in the direction of the ruined court-house, I observed, through the wet, hazy atmosphere, an unusual object in the broken archway, which I at first supposed to be a person stooping down. But, seeing, after the lapse of some minutes, that the object remained stationary, and its posture was unchanged, I took the glass, and, directing it towards the spot, to my great horror I recognised the person of Mr. Gordon, pinioned, and hanging by the neck upon the ruined arch. It was some hours before I recovered from the shock which this sickening spectacle gave me."

Before the hour had fully elapsed which had been allotted to him by the mercy of the military authorities, —not without cause does an old-fashioned book say, " The tender mercies of the wicked are cruel,"—General Nelson appeared, and summoned the condemned man to his fate. He was taken out, and conducted up the steps in front of the court-house; a rope was placed about his neck, the other end being thrown over the crown of the arch. He was then made to mount upon a barrel, which was knocked from under him, and the innocent object of political animosity was cut off from amongst the living. More than twenty other sufferers were strangled at the same time upon a boom running out upon supports from the court-house steps, and others were hung up upon the rails, and the whole left suspended, as was the body of Mr. Gordon, until the following day, when they were thrown all together into a trench dug at the back of the building. The actors in this tragedy may escape the punishment they merit at the hands of man; but the righteous Lord, who loveth righteousness, will not fail to hear the innocent blood which crieth to Him from the ground.

There are several facts testified on oath before the Royal Commissioners, which impart additional shades of darkness to the already dark tragedy of G. W. Gordon's death, beside those which have been already stated. These serve to show how clear and weighty were the

reasons which induced the Jamaica Committee to take
measures for arraigning the principal actors before a
British jury on the charge of murder; not to gratify
any feelings of private revenge, but to vindicate the
outraged law and the tarnished honour of the British
nation.

It has been already related how General Nelson suppressed and destroyed a letter addressed to Mr. Gordon
by Mr. William Wemyss Anderson, of the utmost importance to the accused gentleman, as it was intended
to instruct him how to proceed on the trial, and to
point out the grounds on which he might object to the
jurisdiction of any court-martial in his case. The charge
of the Lord Chief Justice shows that Mr. Anderson's
objections were perfectly valid, and sufficient to bar the
proceedings altogether. But this letter never reached
Mr. Gordon, because General Nelson opened, and read,
and destroyed it; thus deliberately depriving his
prisoner of his last chance for life. This fact is on
record in the Parliamentary papers; and perhaps some
member of the House of Commons may think it due to
the national honour, to inquire if such an act is fitting
and proper in an officer of the British army. Concerning the inhumanity involved in such a procedure
towards a man in jeopardy of his life, there can be but
one opinion.

It is also proved that Mr. Gordon was desirous of
having Dr. Fiddes, or Dr. Major, called at his trial, to
prove that he was out of health at the time of the
Morant Bay outbreak, and that circumstance prevented
his being present at the Vestry meeting which ended so
tragically. The fact of his absence being construed
into proof that he had previous knowledge of what was
to take place, and had therefore purposely kept away
from the meeting, he desired that his medical advisers

might be called, to show that he was at the time physically incapable of being there. Both might have been easily summoned, and certainly would have been if a fair trial had been the object in view. Dr. Major was either at Morant Bay, or so near that a messenger could have reached him in an hour. But with the same disregard of justice and humanity which marked the whole treatment of Mr. Gordon, this reasonable request was refused, and neither of the medical men was allowed to give evidence on a matter so vital to the accused. Thus by the officers who had to do with this impudent mockery of a trial he was deprived of his defence. The following letter, written the day before he was arrested and hurried to Morant Bay to be slaughtered, will explain Mr. Gordon's reason for wishing his medical attendants to be examined. It was addressed to Dr. Fiddes :—

"KINGSTON, *October* 16*th*, 1865.

"MY DEAR DOCTOR,

"THE cough is nearly gone, but the debility of stomach continues ; and I send for some more of the bitters, if you please. Private obloquy is being attached to me about the deplorable occurrences in St. Thomas-in-the-East, but I am as innocent as you are about them. I rather think, if the causes be traced, that the Governor's conduct, and the indiscretion of the late Baron, and judicial proceedings in the parish, will be found to be the real causes. Mr. Eyre has much to answer for in Jamaica affairs.

"Yours faithfully,

"GEORGE WILLIAM GORDON."

It is a very significant circumstance that, when Gordon was to be brought to trial, the court-martial was changed. It had been composed partly of militia officers : and Colonel A. H. Lewis, who had been a political friend of Gordon, had been President of the court

I

sitting at Morant Bay.   But this court was dissolved,
in order that Lieutenant Brand and his two boyish associates might have the disposal of Mr. Gordon's case ;
men whose utter incompetency and unfitness must have
been very well known to General Nelson.   The reason
assigned for making this ominous change was, according
to the Report of the Commissioners, that General Nelson " deemed it right that Mr. Gordon should not be
tried by a court composed of persons who might be supposed to be influenced by local prejudices."   General
Nelson's conduct, in suppressing the letter of Mr. Gordon's legal adviser, renders it very difficult to believe in
any over-anxiety on his part to protect the prisoner
against the influence of " local prejudices ;" nor does it
tend to remove the difficulty that Lieutenant Brand, of
all others, was selected as President of the court.   With
Mr. Lewis as President or even a member of the court,
Mr. Gordon would have had a chance of a fair trial.
But an impartial hearing was out of the question, when
the fate of the accused was placed in the hands of a
man who had boasted of the pleasure he would have in
hanging him, and two associates who were ready with
himself, as the result showed, to send the unfortunate
accused to an ignominious end, on evidence pronounced
by the Lord Chief Justice to be so morally and intrinsically worthless that no competent or honest Judge could
have allowed it to be received.

General Nelson professed to have founded the proceedings in Gordon's trial on his own examination of
Mr. Gordon's papers.   But the fact is, no papers were
found amongst those in the possession of Mr. Gordon,
which could be used against him at the trial ; and none
were so used ; the only documents being depositions of
witnesses not present, a packet abstracted from the post-
office by Ramsay, and two letters, which the evidence
before the Commissioners shows to have been obtained
from other sources.   The most diligent search failed to

discover anything condemnatory of Mr. Gordon, or to connect him, directly or indirectly, with the outbreak at Morant Bay; and it shows how completely his persecutors were at a loss for something to criminate him, that, on the morning of his trial, as proved before the Commissioners, Ramsay, the notorious Provost-marshal, went to the gaol, and proclaimed aloud in the hearing of all the prisoners, " Who can give evidence against Gordon ?   Who knows about Gordon, and can give the evidence against him, will save his life and be rewarded." It would have been strange if, among the host of poor wretches there, every one of whom was in danger of being put to death, there were none found who, prompted by the love of life, would come forward to do what was desired.   Two did come forward : and so it was that, by tendering a bribe to men on the brink of eternity, that miserable testimony was obtained which the Lord Chief Justice pronounces to be moonshine, but which was made the pretext for sending poor Gordon to his death.

Let the conduct of General Nelson be further regarded in connexion with the last act of the tragedy, and how shocking to all right feeling is the inhumanity it discloses !   He had the heartlessness to deny to Mr. Gordon on the verge of eternity what would not be refused to the vilest criminal,—an interview with a minister of religion.   When General Nelson announced to the poor sufferer that his sentence was death, and he was to die in one hour, Mr. Gordon requested to see Mr. Parnther, the Wesleyan Minister in the town, with whom he was on terms of Christian friendship, and at whose house he frequently rested when travelling in that direction.   This request was refused with a cruelty at which one shudders.   Thus defrauded of the counsel of his legal adviser, deprived of the testimony of his medical attendants, and now sternly refused in his last hour the consolations of religion, and the counsels of a Christian Minister, George William Gordon was sent to the gallows. If there be any meaning in the charge of Chief Justice Cockburn, his execution was a murder; and, taking into view all its antecedents and associations, it is as barbarous a murder as can be found in the annals of modern crime. At whose door lies the guilt of this bad deed, will be seen in that day when the Judge of all the earth shall render unto every man according as his work shall be. Meanwhile, conscience will not fail to do its part in punishing the wrong-doers.

Mr. Gordon bore with unruffled meekness the complicated wrongs and indignities to which he was subjected; and even the last crowning act of barbarity, in denying him the consolations of religion, failed to arouse in him any feelings unworthy of a Christian man about to pass within the veil; for immediately after it he sat down, and, with the hand so soon to be stiffened in death, penned a letter to his wife, breathing the same forgiving spirit towards his enemies that his Divine Master exhibited upon the cross, when He prayed for His persecutors, "Father, forgive them; for they know not what they do." This letter, so worthy of a good man's last hour, will long remain a satisfactory memorial of the Christian character and temper of him who wrote it under such harrowing circumstances, and of the repulsive harshness of the British officer who, at such an hour, could refuse such a request. The following is the letter, the ink of which was scarcely dry before the spirit whence it emanated had passed to the better land, "where the wicked cease from troubling, and the weary are at rest."

" MY BELOVED LUCY,

" GENERAL NELSON has just been kind enough to inform me that the court-martial on Saturday last has ordered me to be hung, and that the sentence is to be executed in an hour hence, so that I shall be gone for ever from this world of sin and sorrow. I regret that my worldly affairs are so deranged, but now it cannot be helped. I do not deserve the sentence, for I never advised or took part in any insurrection; all I ever did was to recommend the people who complained, to seek redress in a legitimate way; and if in this I erred, or have been misrepresented, I don't think I deserve this extreme sentence. It is, however, the will of my Heavenly Father that I should thus suffer in obeying His command to relieve the poor and needy, and to protect, so far as I was able, the oppressed; and glory be to His name, and I thank Him that I suffer in such a cause. Glory be to God and Father of our Lord and Saviour Jesus Christ, and I can say that it is a great honour thus to suffer, for the servant cannot be greater than his Lord. I can now say with Paul the aged, 'The hour of my departure it is come, and I am ready to be offered up; I have kept the faith, I have fought a good fight, and henceforth there is laid up for me a crown of righteousness, which the Lord the righteous Judge shall give to me.' Please to say to all my friends an affectionate farewell, and that they must not grieve for me, for I die innocently. Assure Mr. Airey of the truth of this, and all others. Comfort your heart. I certainly little expected this. You must do your best, and the Lord will help you; and do not be ashamed of the death your poor husband will have suffered. The judges seemed against me, and from the rigid manner of the court I could not get in all the explanation I intended. The man Anderson made an unfounded statement: so did Gordon, but his testimony was different from the deposition. The judges took the latter and erased them. It seemed that I was to be sacrificed. I know nothing of Bogle, and never advised him to the act or acts which have brought me to this end. Please to write to Mr. Chamerovzow, Lord Brougham, and Messrs. Henkell, Du Bisson, and Co. I did not expect that, not being a rebel, I should have been tried and disposed of in this way. I thought His Excellency the Governor would have allowed me a fair trial, if any charge of sedition or inflammatory language were partly attributed to me; but I have no power of control. May the Lord be merciful to him! General Nelson, who has just come for me, has faithfully promised to let you have this. May the Lord bless him, and the soldiers and sailors, and all men! Say farewell to Mr. Phillippo, and also Mr. Licard, and aunt, and Mr. Bell, Mr. Vinen, and Mr. Henry Dalouse, and many others whom I do not remember, but who have been true and faithful to me. As the General is come, I must close. Remember me to aunt Eliza in England, and tell her not to be ashamed of my death. And now, my dearest one, the most beloved and faithful, the Lord bless, preserve, and keep you. A kiss for dear mamma, who will be kind to you—to Janet. Kiss also Ann, Janet. Say good bye to dear Mr. Davidson, and all others. I have only been allowed one hour; I wish more time had been allowed. Farewell also to Mr. E. C. Smith, who sent up my private letter to him. And may the grace of our Lord Jesus Christ be with us all!

"Your truly devoted and now nearly dying husband,

"GEORGE W. GORDON.

"I asked to see Mr. Parnther, but the General said I could not. I wish him farewell in Christ. Love to all. Remember aunty and my father. G. W. G."

The Jamaica Committee, with laudable zeal for right and justice, and the security of the life and liberty of British subjects in our colonial possessions, took measures for prosecuting Governor Eyre, General Nelson, and Lieutenant Brand, for the part they respectively took in destroying the life of Mr. Gordon, which they were competently advised amounted legall y in each case to the crime of murder. Mr. Eyre had made it matter of somewhat ostentatious boasting that he took upon himself the entire responsibility of the arrest, trial, and execution of Mr. Gordon; yet, when the time of trial came, with something very much like craven disregard of his own boasting, he shrunk from the responsibility he had assumed, and skulked away from the investigation, which it might have been supposed an honourable man would have courted, and which it is certain that any man, conscious of the rectitude of his own actions and motives, would have been prompt to meet. The Magistrates of Shropshire refused to send the case of Mr. Eyre to a jury, extending over him the shield of their protection by dismissing the case; adding another to those strange examples of "justices' justice" that so often astonish the good people of England. The magistrates in London, faithful to justice and the law, committed Messrs. Nelson and Brand for trial; but the grand jury of Middlesex, to the unbounded astonishment of all who heard or read the charge of the Lord Chief Justice, ignored the bill, and liberated the accused parties from the very serious circumstances in which they were involved. It must have been a mortification deeply and painfully felt by them, to find themselves arraigned at the Old Bailey on the charge of murder. But the attempt to bring the wrong doers to merited punishment, although baffled and defeated by well-understood causes, has not been barren of important and gratifying results. The elaborate charge of Chief Justice Cockburn to the grand jury in the case of Nelson and Brand has supplied what was felt to be a *desideratum*,—a full exposition of the law of England with regard to martial law, and the power of the crown to apply it in the case of civilians. And so fully has he exploded the wild and extravagant doctrines promulgated and acted upon concerning this subject, that no such abuses will ever be practicable again in a British colony as those which recently disgraced Jamaica; while it fixes an indelible stigma upon all concerned in the murder of Mr. Gordon, and the other atrocities perpetrated in the island during the prevalence of martial law. "If," said his Lordship, "the rains of heaven had not washed out the blood from the stones of Jamaica, that blood would cry out for justice."

This is a strong figure of speech, but it contains words of appalling truth. There is reason to believe that the facts as to the amount of life sacrificed in Jamaica, under the sanction of ex-Governor Eyre, and by the agencies he set to work for that purpose, far surpassed what was proved on oath before the Royal Commissioners. After it was seen that the reckless boastings of military and volunteer officers concerning their sanguinary doings amongst the unarmed, unresisting Negroes of Jamaica, called forth no approval of their valour, as they seemed to expect; but, on the contrary, awakened disgust and indignation in the British public to an unexampled extent; they dropped their ill-timed braggadocio, and endeavoured, by contrary representations, to counteract the effect produced. No doubt everything was done before the Commissioners that could possibly minify the havoc and bloodshed which had taken place, and give the most favourable aspect to the whole case. But if we take it just as it is represented in the official Report of the Commissioners, it presents an appalling record of human wickedness, and casts a fearful amount of responsibility upon Mr. Eyre, such as most men would shudder to contemplate, in the view of having to appear with it, and confront it, before the judgment-seat of Christ.

It will be remembered that before the hanging and shooting commenced, the so-called rebellion had been suppressed. Not one of the numerous victims of the martial law frenzy was killed in actual resistance to authority : every one was massacred in cold blood, and in a fiendish spirit of revenge. In the heat of conflict, the Negroes, exasperated to fury by a wanton attack made upon them with deadly weapons, killed eighteen persons and wounded thirty-one. Twenty houses or stores were wholly or partially plundered, and five buildings, including the court-house and school-house at Morant Bay, and a house at Mulatto River, accidentally set on fire, were burnt. But on the part of the authorities there were, on the day of the riot at Morant Bay, ten killed and twenty wounded by the fire of the volunteers; four hundred and thirty-nine are proved to have been afterwards put to death (a number, there is reason to fear, very far short of the reality); six hundred were tortured by the cat, many of them with the fearful instrument of cruelty made partly of ironwire; and a thousand houses were wantonly burnt, leaving four thousand of the labouring population without a shelter or a home. It is not surprising that the Royal Commissioners say in the conclusion of their Report :—

"By the continuance of martial law in its full force to the extreme limit of its statutory operation, the people were deprived for a longer time than the necessary period of the great constitutional privileges by which the security of life and property is provided for. That the punishments inflicted were excessive. That the punishment of death was unnecessarily frequent. That the floggings were reckless, and at Bath positively barbarous. That the burning of one thousand houses was wanton and cruel."

Lord Chief Justice Cockburn has conferred a benefit upon the world by publishing his admirable charge in a volume, with his own revision and corrections and copious notes. The following remarks close the volume, and present such a lucid view of the barbarity and illegality with which Mr. Gordon was treated, that it is impossible to read them, and remember that they proceed from the highest legal authority in the realm, without regarding Mr. Gordon as a murdered man, and feeling that a most unenviable responsibility will to the end of their lives, and beyond that period, attach to the men by whom he was cruelly and unlawfully done to death. The Chief Justice says :—

" English legislation, looking, no doubt, to the disadvantage a man labours under who has the power of Government to contend with, and to the danger of angry passions and hostile prejudices interfering with the calm administration of justice on trials for treason, has provided additional safeguards for the protection of the accused. The prisoner, in addition to the right to have copies of the depositions as on ordinary trials, has by statute (7 Anne, c. xi., s. 21) the right to have a copy of the indictment delivered to him a fortnight before the trial, together with a list of the witnesses to be produced against him, as well as a list of the jury. On opening the 'Times' of May 1st, my eye alighted on the following passage from a report of the proceedings against the Fenian prisoners at Dublin :—

"' Mr. Justice Fitzgerald' sat half an hour before the usual time yesterday morning, in order to assign counsel to prisoners against whom true bills had been found for high treason. When they were placed at the bar, his Lordship informed them that the grand jury had found bills of indictment against them for high treason. They were entitled to copies of the indictment, which would be furnished them either to-day or to-morrow, as also lists of the jurors and witnesses. They would be called upon to plead to the indictment found against them on Monday, the 13th of May. He had further to tell them that they were entitled to name two counsel and an attorney to act for them. If they were not prepared to do that then, they could name the professional gentlemen they wished to represent them at any time between that and the 13th of May to the Governor of the prison, who would communicate their wishes to the Crown Solicitor.'

" Contrast this with the proceedings in Mr. Gordon's case. Taken from a place where he would have had the advantage of a regular trial, a previous knowledge of the case he had to meet, the means of defence, the presence of friends, the assistance of counsel, the cross-examination of the witnesses, the full opportunity to rebut their testimony by counter-evidence; the direction to the jury of a professional and responsible Judge, he is hurried off without an opportunity of communicating with any one, and transported to another part of the island, where he had neither friend nor adviser. Even a letter written to him by a friend, suggesting the line of defence, is purposely kept from him. Alone and helpless, he is immediately, and with unseemly and deplorable haste, put upon his trial, without knowledge of the charge till called upon to answer it, without knowledge of the facts intended to be proved, or of the witnesses intended to be examined, still less that the depositions of living witnesses taken behind his back would be brought forward against him. Under these most disadvantageous circumstances he is put upon his trial, before a court, in all probability, sharing in the common prepossession against him, and is condemned on evidence, in my judgment, wholly insufficient to warrant his condemnation. It may be said, it is true, that Gordon did not apply for a postponement of the trial. But of what advantage would a postponement have been to him, while in total ignorance of what he had to meet? Besides which, this unhappy man appears, if one may judge from the utter want of vigour and intelligence displayed in his defence, to have been paralysed by the circumstances in which he was placed, and to have been rendered incapable of grappling with the difficulties by which he was surrounded. No one, I think, who has the faintest idea of what the administration of justice involves, could deem the proceedings on this trial consistent with justice, or, to use a homely phrase, with that fair play which is the right of the commonest criminal. All I can say is, that if, on martial law being proclaimed, a man can lawfully be thus tried, condemned, and sacrificed, such a state of things is a scandal and a reproach to the institutions of this great and free country; and as a minister of justice, profoundly imbued with a sense of what is due to the first and greatest of earthly obligations, I enter my solemn and emphatic protest against the lives of men being thus dealt with in time to come."

It was some satisfaction to the public mind that Mr. Eyre was promptly dismissed from the government of

Jamaica, and deprived of the authority he had so grossly abused. And it is scarcely possible that any administration can venture so to outrage public opinion and propriety, as to place him again in a similar position of responsibility. But it is still more satisfactory to know, that no West India Governor will be able, in future, to shelter himself under any local enactment in placing a colony under martial law, and that all local laws on that subject have been ordered to be effaced from the statute book; so that henceforth no Governor can proclaim martial law, except on his own personal responsibility,—a responsibility so stupendous that it will seldom, if ever, be incurred; especially after the exposition of the law on the subject given by Chief Justice Cockburn. It is also a pleasing fact that a new system of administration has been inaugurated in misgoverned Jamaica, which bids fair to produce a better and more equitable state of things than that which for so many years has existed in that colony. Some of the reforms which Mr. Gordon advocated, and laboured long to accomplish, are now in progress. The present Governor, Sir J. P. Grant, armed with powers almost despotic, is repealing and altering oppressive laws, rendering the burden of taxation more equal amongst rich and poor, cutting down the enormous expense of the Church establishment, and providing for such a fair and impartial administration of the laws as shall obviate just ground of complaint; and we trust the day is not far distant, when the peasantry of Jamaica, released from the oppressions by which they have been ground to the earth, will be amongst the most prosperous and happy classes of Her Majesty's subjects.

LONDON:
PRINTED BY WILLIAM NICHOLS,
46, HOXTON SQUARE.

CPSIA information can be obtained at www.ICGtesting.com
Printed in the USA
LVOW03s2302220114

370540LV00015B/725/P